Allotment
Manual

First published in March 2012

A catalogue record for this book is available from the British Library

ISBN 978 0 85733 160 1

Published by Haynes Publishing,
Sparkford, Yeovil, Somerset BA22 7JJ, UK
Tel: 01963 442030 Fax: 01963 440001
Int. tel: +44 1963 442030 Int. fax: +44 1963 440001
E-mail: sales@haynes.co.uk
Website: www.haynes.co.uk

Haynes North America Inc.
861 Lawrence Drive, Newbury Park,
California 91320, USA

Printed in the USA by Odcombe Press LP,
1299 Bridgestone Parkway, La Vergne, TN 37086

Credits

Author:	**Paul Peacock**
Project Manager:	**Louise McIntyre**
Copy editor:	**Jane Hutchings**
Page design:	**Rod Teasdale**
Photography:	**Paul Peacock, Glow Images, istockphoto.**

The publishers would like to thank Steve Ott, Joyce Russell and Ben Russell for their contributions.

Allotment
Manual

Paul Peacock

CONTENTS

INTRODUCTION

You do not have to be a prophet or a seer to realise the importance of allotments. Without delving too deeply into the economics of the modern world, or into the other problems that are putting pressure on our ability to grow food, it is becoming obvious that people in the West will not be able to rely on imported food forever.

Food supply is not meeting demand, perhaps for the first time. Pollution, desertification, changes in weather systems, increasing pressure on water, fertility problems and expanding population join together to create a grim picture. Some researchers are saying that in future farming will take place in Western cities.

Clearly the world of allotments has an important role to play in providing people with a small amount of land and a huge opportunity to grow some food. But there is more to it than that – allotments are special places.

When you step onto an allotment, everything changes. You enter a horizontal world of green, where smells excite the mind and growing fruit and vegetables whets the

appetite. You enter a democracy in microcosm, a place where people matter, decisions are generally by consensus and a high sense of ownership settles everyone.

Plot-holders might never talk to their neighbours at home, but there is always time for a chat on the plot. Highlights include a cup of tea in the clubhouse, a show where prizes might seem elusive but are well merited in the end, the aroma of Jeyes Fluid in winter and work parties that help newcomers or repair paths and fences.

The allotment is a place where people can work together, learn how to live in a complex world (where else can a boy and a man work alongside for a day these days?) and prepare and grow the best food there could possibly be.

This is the crux of the allotment for me. It is a place where the very best peas and potatoes, tomatoes and peppers, cabbages and leeks are grown. It is great to see an allotment full of roses, or chrysanthemums or dahlias, but a plot full of onions, cabbages and potatoes – you cannot get better.

I know they say frozen peas are just as good as fresh ones, possibly better! However, when you have watched them grow, watered and fed them, podded and cooked them, there is something that the freezer aisle in the supermarket cannot provide: pride in your own handiwork. And that is the best seasoning you could ever wish for.

If you are unable to buy land to grow food for your family, rent an allotment. It is probably the best thing you could do for your loved ones, especially in these difficult times.

Allotments have become a political force. There are associations to join, magazines to read, and when the government wanted to alter the way councils provided allotments, thousands responded by lobbying officials. Ministers changed their tune within a week. The cry 'Hands off our allotments' was read in newspapers and heard in Parliament and council chambers around the country.

This book looks to how to get, grow, maintain and run an allotment. Hopefully it might send a further message: 'Hands off our allotments' could become 'Hands on our allotments', because, more than ever, we need more. During the Second World War there were 5 million allotments. Today we need to increase our current provision 40-times to reach that figure and we need to be ready to make allotments wherever we can.

If you don't have one, keep pressing, and if you do – enjoy! The soil of your plot is possibly the most important thing you have.

Happy allotmenting!

History

Everywhere you go around the United Kingdom you find allotments. There are just as many in the countryside, with its apparent expanse of land, as there are in the town and city, where land is at a premium. No one really knows how many allotments there are, but the number of people wanting one has never been higher. Allotments are more popular now than at their peak in the Second World War, when more than 5 million were in cultivation.

Originally, the allotment was in the gift of the church, offering just about enough land to grow wheat for a family for a year, so long as they gleaned the fields to add to their supply. Vegetables were garden plants, grown at home, and to this day there appears to be a difference in the allotmenteer's mind, between the plants grown at home and on the 'lottie'.

Allotments grew in number, if not size, through the Victorian period, when the growing of food became more important in the cities. Local towns and cities saw allotments as a way of helping the poor help themselves. In northern towns where, during the Great Famine caused by the successive failure of the potato crop in Ireland, millions of Irish swelled urban numbers, communities could no longer cope. Huge areas of park and common land were ripped up to make allotments.

At the same time, recreation parks, libraries and day schools were hastily provided, along with sewerage and clean water. Consequently, allotments became associated with the liberalisation of the UK and the provision of social structures that made urban life not only bearable but safe, both in terms of health and well-being.

Allotments at the turn of the 19th century were one of the great strengths of the nation, and a series of support structures grew up alongside them. Their inexpensive rent together with a popular gardening press, thousands of growing competitions for both flowers and vegetables at local, city, regional and national levels, and plenty of social interaction brought a little of country life within reach of the working poor.

Allotments were seen to be so important to the socio-economic fabric of the country that the government passed a law in 1909 forcing local authorities to provide allotments, or at least to investigate the provision, if there were none available, for a minimum number in an area that needed them.

One would have thought that the allotment, as portrayed by the urban societies that created them, had always been with us. Generally, there was something masculine about them, a little like the tap room of the local pub, a place of boyhood rite of passage, strange smells of Jeyes Fluid, sheds and topless figures. But this vision of the allotment was little over 50 years old when the Local Government Act made its provision compulsory.

Before the widespread dash to create local authority allotments, they were individually owned, sometimes by the parish council, sometimes by churches, pubs, collieries, cotton mills, soap and chemical manufacturers. Each had their own peculiarities, some were little more than scraped fields, others were magnificent affairs with clubhouses and were the centre of benevolent welfare from their employers. Often, in the early days, they were also the only place where workers could 'buy' food and groceries with the tokens given to them instead of real money.

The First World War saw a fundamental change in allotmenting. With husbands and sons away, it was left largely to women to take over not only factory chores, but allotments too. Pigeons, hens and bees, goats and pigs were all commonplace on allotments, in an age before overt regulation, and the women found themselves occupying their men's places. They were indeed the forerunner of the Land Girl's movement of the Second World War.

The allotment became a place of solace following the First World War, generally recognised for keeping people fit and fed during a dreadful time of food shortages and influenza; a time when more people died in their beds of Spanish Flu than in the trenches a couple of years earlier. Still, the numbers of plots increased during the 1920s and 1930s, through depression and austerity.

It was, however, the *Dig for Victory* campaign of the Second World War that attracted the most attention. A super piece of propaganda, the campaign had several effects. It brought people together. Five million allotments all but fed the nation, and fed it well. They brought a sense of purpose to non-combatants at a time when it was said the country never had more than a couple of weeks of food in reserve. The nation did not become fully self-sufficient during that time, but it was approaching it. The model of allotments for all remains a dream for many today – partly an ideological one

since there are barely a tenth of the allotments of war-time Britain – but for a few short years it seemed possible.

The years after the war remained austere, with rationing and urban poverty, but it was during these years that allotments started to decline. Temporary allotments were returned to their original uses. Those built on bomb sites (and there were quite a few) were reclaimed, as were those built on public amenity and parkland.

Increased productivity caused Prime Minister Harold Macmillan to claim 'we never had it so good' and increased wealth meant people bought food rather than grew it. Supermarkets started in the 1960s, and from then on people found it easier to buy fruit and vegetables.

The social aspect of allotments seemed to become less relevant for ordinary people. They became the quaint, flat-capped, old-fashioned world of irascible elderly gentlemen and domineering committees, at a time when gardening itself was changing.

As surely as the Second World War changed the way we gardened for food, the advent of television changed the way we gardened completely. Sick of austerity, people loved the popular gardening programmes. *Garden Club* and later *Gardeners' World* emphasised the aspirational side of gardening. Instead of the urban version of the cottage garden, the growing of prize-winning flowers and vegetables, people

planted lawns and filled borders with the most popular flowers and maybe grew a few vegetables. The supermarket replaced the veg plot and the allotment failed to move with the times.

Local authorities turned many allotments into swing parks, schools, roads, old folks' homes and housing estates. Perceived public health concerns led to many authorities banning livestock; hens and pigeons had to go and government implementation of increasingly harsh agricultural requirements to combat many diseases, including foot-and-mouth disease, caused the demise of the goat for allotmenteers, and the complete withdrawal of the pig.

Renaissance of the allotment

Likely as not driven by television programmes, a growing number of people want to change the way they feed themselves. The movement for allotments is largely reactionary: people do not want chemicals in their food, they do want high standards of culture and animal welfare. They instinctively react against supermarkets, and maintain the food they grow tastes better and is healthier than anything provided by the chains. They desire homelier, more nourishing and better food, but there is more to it than that.

The companies behind supermarkets and restaurant chains, producing packaged, pre-cooked food, will say that their products are safe, wholesome, and wonderfully tasty. They might point out there is no difference between a carrot (or anything else for that matter) grown in a field and one pampered in a raised bed. Although what they say might be true, for the estimated million-plus people waiting to get their first allotment, that is not the point. They want to produce their own food. Even if this has to be topped up from the shops, their carrots are tastier because they are *their* carrots. Pride is the best seasoning you can get.

There is another side to the modern allotment. The celebration of all things natural and organic has invaded our plots; people are not only growing and eating their own produce, they are exploring new experiences like keeping hens and bees and the world of the allotment is fast fulfilling the social needs of those who have them.

Allotments are changing. No longer the watchtower of the flat-capped brigade, the common feature is youth. Parents expose children to healthier living through having an allotment, schools have allotments, as do community groups. Allotments have wildlife areas, and liaison officers bring the community inside the gates. Some local authorities allow allotments sites to sell food direct to the public and the

issue of food miles and access to locally produced food are high on planning agendas around the country.

With all this, the running of allotments has become a political issue. When there was a hint that the government was considering relaxing the law that gives local authorities the duty to provide allotments, thousands threw up their hands in complaint. Allotment-holders collected 1,500 signatures in a few days and the prime minister was forced to go public in Parliament to say such a change would never be contemplated. Stories were published in the *Daily Mail* and the *Independent* and allotmenteers ran a campaign that in the space of a couple of weeks changed government policy.

The hundreds of thousands who run allotments, from the 'Hon. Secretary' to those on the waiting list looking patiently for signs of neglect in any corner of the site, to the many more non-gardening members who buy compost and fertiliser from the association shop – usually a shed or Portakabin – have found more than a garden, more than a place to grow food. They have found a society, culture, friendship, a cause, a whole way of life down on the plot, and this book is dedicated to them.

FINDING AN ALLOTMENT

New allotments take time to develop

You would be forgiven for thinking, in some circumstances, that people would be put off from getting an allotment by the strange unwritten laws that everyone on the site, other than you, have known and obeyed from infancy.

My allotmenting days started with a prescription from my doctor. I had blood pressure that would kill a horse and he was a practical joker. He gave me a prescription that I didn't read and in turn I passed on to the chemist. The chemist came out of the back of the shop and handed me a box of pills. "I can't fulfil the rest of the prescription, we don't stock it." With a wry smile he handed me the prescription which read:

Staryl 15 mg. Tabs.
One allotment, dug daily as prescribed.

I decided to take him up on his remedy and get an allotment.

Turning up one Sunday morning I found 'Hon. Secretary' in his greenhouse, where I enquired if I could have a plot. I was in luck. An old chap had retired from his, and I could have that, No. 14, over the far side.

I followed the path to where I thought No. 14 was. Next to it was a broken-down shed and a small rubbish tip, bicycle frames, corrugated iron, a complete mess. I was not impressed to find the mess was actually my allotment, not the one I had hoped for. Gloomily I started to clear some of the rubbish away only to find Hon. Secretary running along the path. He was red-faced and shouting what I thought I was doing. It turned out that I was not allowed to touch the plot until I had paid 'Old Bill' for his shed.

You can get a lot of information from websites.

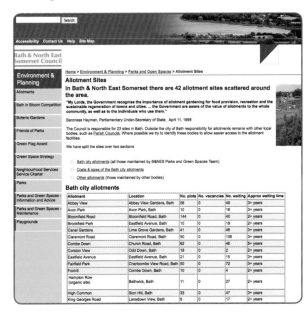

'Where does he live?'
'Dunno!'

He took a lot of finding did 'Old Bill', but he said I could have the shed for free; all he wanted from it was his ton dish and old riddle. I didn't know what he was on about but I promised to keep my eye open.

Back on the plot, I started to shift the rubbish. Everyone seemed to know I had seen Bill and one by one they strolled along to help me clear the plot. Sometimes obeying the unwritten rules is a rite of passage.

This was my introduction to allotmenteering. It is not untypical and you have to remember that the world of allotments is not the same as the world of gardening, partly because the allotment is a community of gardeners, partly because the allotment is a long-standing public association that has to have safeguards and transparency.

Getting an allotment can be at times a little unusual, so spend some time asking questions. We will come back to this later.

How to get an allotment

First, and most importantly, look around. If you are new to an area, ask your neighbours where the nearest allotments can be found. In some localities you might find the allotments nearest to you are provided by a different local authority. In rare cases you may not be allowed to become a member if you live in a different authority area, but the majority of allotments will accept you if you live within reasonable walking distance.

If all else fails, information about allotments can be found on your council website or at your local library. Often it is worth a trip to your library anyway, because the local knowledge of the library staff will tell you things that a website can't, such as parking, bus routes, and exactly where they are (the most important information of all!).

For more information about allotments and how they might meet your needs, phone your local allotments officer – there is usually at least one in each authority. He or she will be able to give you the state of allotments and which ones are best to apply to. If you need disabled access, the allotments officer should be your first point of call.

Visit the allotment

Almost invariably the best time to visit the allotment to find a plot is about 11am on Sunday morning. There are bound to be some committee members on site. You may find the gates locked, but a quick shout will soon bring someone to let you in.

Many allotments have open days, so turning up will bring you a guided tour, maybe a burger and a taste of home-made jam on a scone, a cup of tea and the chance to buy some produce.

Should I join?

Things to look out for include:

- **The state of the perimeter fence** Security is really important, and if people are constantly gaining access to the site, it is usually because someone has left the gate open and unlocked.
- **Are the paths tidy?** Is there lots of plant material lying around? Allotments that are strict about issues such as not allowing material to rot on paths are frequently better places to be.
- **Are the sheds tidy and well maintained?** Allotments have differing rules about sheds. Some say they must be kept in line, others do not bother about them. One sure thing is they should not be used as a store for tools and, if you are able, leave the door unlocked.
- **Is there a toilet?** Having to go to the toilet in your shed is not acceptable. If there are a couple of Portaloos, or better still a clubhouse with a toilet, do they smell? Are they clean, and do you feel comfortable in there?
- **Clubhouse** Is there a good brew station? You can tell a sociable allotment by the number of cups, and washed ones at that! Is the clubhouse clean and tidy, and is there a shop?
- **Social events** A good calendar of social events is an important indicator. If the plot-holders like socialising together you can more or less guarantee there are few issues among them.

Look at other allotments to get ideas and growing hints.

How societies are arranged

We will look at how committees are arranged elsewhere (*see Allotments Officers page 19*), but for now we need to say something about the apparent confusion surrounding the organisation of some allotments.

The Ramsbottom Horticultural Society, for instance, can be found in a shed on allotments in Ramsbottom, Lancashire. The society 'runs' the allotments alongside the council, a convenient marriage between the two (and what a lovely site it is). Joining the horticultural society does not mean you are entitled to an allotment, far from it. It may be possible, but unlikely, to rent an allotment from the council without joining the society.

COMMUNITY SPIRIT

Running an allotments society is first and foremost a community affair. Some management committees focus on the look of the allotments, some on the finances, others on the state of the plots and improvements, still others on combating vandalism. All these are important aspects of running an allotments site. However, remembering the site is a community of people, rather than a series of gardens, will keep it an attractive and enjoyable place to be.

Non-gardening member

The first thing to do to get an allotment is to become a non-gardening member. Even if this step is unnecessary, it shows your commitment, and more. For a nominal fee you can use the shop, get discounts on gardening supplies and enter the shows.

Then get yourself on the waiting list for a plot. It won't be long before you find out about the plot-holders: who are the best ones for advice, who is planning to leave, and who would be willing to share their plot with you. You would be surprised how many long-standing plot-holders want to keep their plots, but are no longer up to the task of keeping their garden in good shape, and a little help from you will mean you will learn a lot about good, old-fashioned gardening.

The community plot

Many sites have community plots that need help in their upkeep. School plots have to be tended during the holidays and other community areas need working on too. Some societies have wildlife areas, which require special care or allotmenteers may complain about weed seeds landing on their plot.

Community areas are a good place for you to volunteer and do some gardening. Your keenness and commitment will be rewarded with your ultimate goal – your own allotment.

What can I expect when I get an allotment?

Many allotment societies are now splitting vacant allotments into a smaller units and it is likely you will be offered half a plot as your first garden. There is logic behind this: often people want allotments without realising how much work there is maintaining a plot, and it is far less troublesome to the committee if you decide to give up your half plot. It is also a form of mutual probation, and if you have kept up your gardening regime well, you will be able to transfer to a full plot should one become available.

Charges

When you first join the allotments you will be asked to pay some fees, including:

- a key deposit, usually between £5 and £10
- a water rates charge
- an annual subscription, or the pro rata rate up until when the fees are due for the next year

You can never start too early.

■ a sum for anything that is on your allotment, such as a shed or greenhouse. It is here that you make your impression on the society for the first time. Sheds on allotments are inexpensive, and in most cases the committee will make sure there is little or nothing to pay by agreement with the previous tenant. However, if you are benefiting from a good shed, a modest donation to the club funds is always useful. If you cannot afford to pay, say so, the committee will sort things out for you. There is always someone on the site who needs a cheap greenhouse or shed.

Discounts If you are a pensioner, or if you are unemployed, or a student, you should receive a rebate on your fees – or even the full amount. If your plot is badly overgrown, then a rent-free period of grace is often allowed. A good allotments site will have fellow plot-holders working on your new plot both before and after you arrive.

Some things you need to know
The site will have policies and you should be given a list of these, otherwise it is always worth finding out.

■ **Paths** Which paths are you responsible for and what is required?

■ **Sheds and buildings** Do you have to place sheds and greenhouses in line with the others, and is there a colour code?

■ **Water** Is there a hosepipe policy or a water-butt policy? Is the site uniformly drained and are there plans to drain your plot if it is too wet, or do you have to do it yourself?

■ **Gate policy** This is the frustration of all allotment-holders. Gates left unlocked invite vandals, and this is one of the most frustrating jobs the committee has to deal with – getting people to lock the gate. You need to find out!

■ **Compost** Some sites insist you make compost on your plot, others insist you add your garden waste to the site compost heap. This also applies to the delivery of farmyard manure.

■ **Parking** Always observe the parking rules. If you need to drive to your plot – and everyone needs to from time to time to unload – remove your car as quickly as possible.

■ **Tools** Most plots have a shed full of tools for communal use. Be sure to find out exactly what you can use. Often you will find tools – Rotavators for example – that belong to someone and are just there for safe keeping. Always clean tools when you have used them and, if you can, put them back in the same place you found them. There may be a booking-out system, and if you have used a petrol machine, make sure you replace the fuel.

■ **Fuel** Some allotments have a charging system for fuel, rather than having lots of different people filling the fuel cans. Also, some leave fuel in the machine, others empty it out. Ask whoever is in charge about what you have to do when you borrow.

KEEP IN TOUCH

There are lots of ways of communicating with other plot-holders. First, there is sure to be a member adept with computers. A weekly newsletter (or a monthly one) is a fine way of increasing the community spirit. Avoid lists of dos and don'ts and who has transgressed where. Focus on people's news, what they are doing on their plots, calls to arms (working parties), birthdays, sicknesses and so on.

If you can get your allotment on the Internet, all the better – people have a great time sharing their hobby on Facebook – and allotments are a growing part of this. You don't need web space or even a subscription, just a computer. Your members will do the rest as they log on, add their news and photographs, and the community spirit will be there for all to see.

Increase the fertility of the plot by adding compost.

THE ALLOTMENT WORLD

Allotments are full of wonder – especially at harvest!

Allotments are communities of like-minded people, each of them tending a garden. The garden is the main reason for them being there – some need to grow cheap food, others grow flowers and ornamental plants. Some grow as a part of a healthy, self-sufficient lifestyle and others grow because they need room for fruit, or to keep hens or bees.

All of these people belong to a community, and the allotments should be set up in such a way as to cater for their needs. Concentrating on the gardens alone will not produce the best of allotments, but concentrating on the gardeners will.

THE GOLDEN RULE

Everyone on the site is an amateur. He or she does this because they love it, and gives their time freely. Consequently, whereas they do have responsibilities regarding their position in the management team, these responsibilities should never be onerous, nor should there be any element of pressure or failure.

Tasks should be tackled with partners, and support should come from at least two other sections of the community. For example, the annual show organiser should be backed up by a deputy, and in the arrangement of shows should have the practical help of the publicity liaison officer, the trophies officer, the gardening advisers, the maintenance crew, the newsletter secretary and so on. Nothing should be loaded on a single person.

Ownership – it's everyone's site

Allotments can be said to be democracy in micro, and the way to give people ownership of the allotments is to be sure everyone has a role and something to contribute. Let's be honest, there are allotments out there where no one ventures off their plot, nor speaks to their neighbour. And you can tell them, too! Unwelcoming, unfriendly, burdened by rules, a place that takes some determination to keep a

plot going. Some allotments buzz with activity, events, socials, fêtes and fairs, competitions and the sound of chatter. There are brew times and food, families and fun.

The allotments are also a resource for the locality and one could extend the ownership argument to the people living nearby. Some allotments societies have taken this to heart and reach out to the local community either directly or via the local school, doctor's surgery, supermarket or other group.

Community course in action in an allotment society shed. People here are learning how to keep bees.

The committee meeting doesn't have to be in the shed!

Allotments officers

The allotments officers are representatives for the site and its plot-holders. It is their job to discuss, plan and generally manage the site and to formulate decisions. The secretary and treasurer are the only two 'offices' you need for an allotments group, though most allotments seem to have different ways of adding more members to the committee. Usually the methodology is set down in the constitution, which originally provided the legal framework for the allotment. Some groups have a simple list of committee members, others have set roles that may include a president, show secretary, maintenance officers and people to cover publicity, produce a newsletter and organise social events.

Secretary

The secretary (sometimes known as the hon. secretary) chairs meetings and ensures the minutes of the meetings are accurate and up-to-date to the satisfaction of all concerned. The secretary deals with queries and complaints from both inside the allotments or from outside. The role includes overall management and provides back-up for the other officers.

Treasurer

The treasurer maintains bank accounts and keeps a record of receipts, payments and anything financial. In addition, the treasurer:

■ has the role of collecting rents and paying them to the council (or landlord) – it should not be the treasurer's sole responsibility to chase people for rent arrears.
■ deals with the other outgoings, such as water rates, fence repairs, payments for key-cutting and ensuring there is enough money to repay deposits when plot-holders leave.

TOP FIVE JOBS FOR THE SECRETARY

1 To listen to plot-holders, to get to know them, to see their plots and talk gardening, to act on disputes.
2 To represent the allotments in wider forums, such as at council meetings, allotments' officer meetings, grant meetings.
3 To maintain the smooth running of the processes of the plots and the society as a whole.
4 To spearhead the direction of the society with the committee.
5 To initiate and progress grants applications.

TOP FIVE JOBS FOR THE TREASURER

1 To aid the secretary and committee with financial information.
2 To help collect and monitor rents and other income and pay various bills.
3 To advise on funding requirements against society funds.
4 To listen to plot-holders' views on the needs of the plots and suggest remedies, especially where funding is required.
5 To produce reports for public approval, viewing and auditing.

19

Always time for a cuppa and a chat.

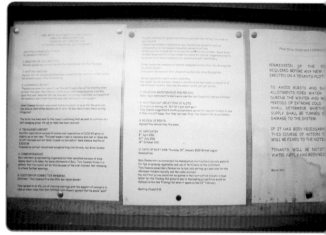

The very least you need is a notice board to communicate with gardeners.

President (and deputy)

This is often someone who has local standing in the community, who is both well known and has plenty of contacts. Sometimes it is a local councillor, other times it is a celebrity gardener. The president of the society is largely an honorary role, representing the group in a wider way than the committee can normally do. Sometimes the office of president is given as an honour, a distinction for long service or achievement. If your group has such an office, the roles and responsibilities should be clearly set out in the constitution, along with the rules for choosing the officer and the length of term.

Show secretary

The show secretary does not work alone. Running the annual (or more) show is a complex affair, requiring the cooperation of a number of people. We will look at organising shows and open days later in this book, but the show secretary has overall responsibility for the event and needs to be a strong character because it can be notoriously difficult to please everyone. In some societies shows are combined with open days.

■ The main tool of the show secretary is the schedule. This is a list of entrants, a rule book and a timetable all rolled into one. It needs to be produced well in advance of the event so gardeners can prepare themselves and their exhibits. The rules should be clear and easy to understand, with no room for ambiguity. For example, the entry for onions might read 'Five identical cropped onions on a plate'. Where there is need for explanation, it should be given.

■ Show secretary is a complex task and should be given to a person who has a deal of experience, preferably of judging as well as organising. The officer should also have a number of contacts in the local community, including judges, as well as the ability to source prizes and trophies (many societies also have a trophies secretary).

Publicity and newsletter secretaries

The roles of these secretaries are often combined since a newsletter can also be used as publicity material. The publicity secretary does not need many skills, save the ability to phone the local newspaper, but it helps to be imaginative and to have a decent camera – newspapers love pictures. The newsletter secretary has a number of functions and the fact that information has to be collected from different people affords the possibility of some coordination (see Keep in touch, page 15).

■ Societies use publicity to get their projects known in their community; some advertise their open days, shows and association shop in the local press and in shop windows and on community notice boards.

■ Many societies share information about break-ins (anyone offered tools in the local pub might know where they came from) and vandalism reports. This is particularly useful when asking the local councillor for help to access funding, because it is one of the markers for giving grants to socially deprived areas. If you can include the politician in your press release, it may boost your case.

■ The ability to make best advantage of social media is becoming more important. Many allotments societies have followings all over the country.

■ Most allotments groups are members of the National Society of Allotment and Leisure Gardeners (NSALG), and other bodies. Often magazines are received by the committee but no one else ever sees them. Maintaining the supply and distribution of these publications and, if possible, the allotments library is an enormously valuable task.

Fences and paths officer

Usually not solely confined to fences and paths, this officer is responsible for maintenance around the site *(see Maintenance – what's what, page 24)*. In most cases the perimeter fencing of allotments is the joint responsibility of the management committee and the local council. Internal fences and paths are always the sole responsibility of the management committee. The fences and paths officer has responsibility for:

- the coordination of working parties
- creating suitable areas for farmyard manure, which will ruin a path if left on concrete
- the general tidiness of the allotments
- ensuring that gardeners are sticking to the rules where they refer to the material of the site. *Gentle reminders being the rule of the day!*

Shop committee

There is no reason why the local allotments shop, selling seeds, fertilisers, pots and so on, cannot become the main provider of gardening materials to members, including those who are on the waiting list. The shop committee has the task of running the enterprise, buying materials from wholesalers, taking money and manning the shop. The officers need to be independent and settled, putting money into the society's coffers, while at the same time being in post for long enough to ensure continuity of supply.

Paths are the most important part of an allotment, and define a good site from a bad one.

The shop is for the site and the wider community.

You just can't get better advice than from people who have been gardening for a long time.

Social secretary

Everything from providing a brew in the clubhouse, shed or polytunnel, to a full-blown barn dance, to helping the show secretary, is the responsibility of the social secretary. It is often the social secretary who is the licence holder if the association has a bar.

Tools secretary

Every society has a stock of tools, some more than others. The tools secretary is responsible for the booking in and out of tools, the fitness and maintenance of the equipment (especially if there are any power tools in the shed), the shed itself and the availability of fuel (which needs to be reimbursed by the users). It is a good idea to keep fuel separate and off-site if possible, and provided to gardeners on a pre-

arranged basis. One allotment-holder was known to keep fuel in a tin can, inside an ammunition box that was cleverly buried inside his muck heap – no one would have thought of messing with it there.

Livestock secretary

Many local authorities do not allow livestock on their sites, though we should remember the reason for allotments and allow at least hens and bees to be kept as a matter of right. The role of the livestock officer is to liaise with owners and the local authority, and to maintain the proper paperwork, or at least get the owners to do so.

Ensuring the correct insurances are in place – especially for beekeeping – is really important and that the livestock is not a nuisance to other gardeners or people off-site (no cockerels heralding a 4.14am dawn for example).

NSALG secretary

This person makes the gardeners aware of trends, news, shows and so on from the various bodies with which the society is associated – the Rose Society, for instance. There is always something new to be learned in allotmenting and there is also something both quaint and right about gardeners supporting as many gardening societies as possible.

Garden instructors

This is a happy band of uncles and aunts who give a helping hand to new gardeners. Some plots are so friendly you don't need such a post, but to be honest, there never was a plot spoiled by having them. The idea behind the office is for people to wander and chat about gardening, and also to provide a resource for anyone on the plot to come and ask questions.

Schools and public liaison

The role of allotments is changing. There are often funds available for public liaison, and local authorities sometimes put money into expanding the resource of places like allotments to benefit the community.

Public liaison can do a lot of good in the catchment area of allotments, but can also create a lot of work. Bringing people into the gardens for a walk around means the plots and paths have to be well maintained. Many allotments organise luncheon clubs, schools visits, gardening classes, bingo and other social clubs, and open public plots that anyone can come and garden. An allotments group in Rochdale, Lancashire, had a building created with a shop so the society could sell vegetables direct to the public whenever they were available, donated by plot-holders. Such an idea opens many doors and sources of income on the one hand, and brings many problems on the other, including the need for a shop committee.

Local authority

It might be the secretary (hon. secretary) who deals with matters at local authority level. Many local authorities have an overall allotments' society, such as the Association of Manchester Allotment Societies (AMAS), which offers a programme of events, shows, lectures and a combined stand at Tatton Park RHS Show. Clearly, no such association is possible without a large amount of support from individual societies.

Choosing your representatives

The best time is to renew officers annually by secret ballot at an event. If you have a newsletter, all the candidates should be posted in it, and on a suitable notice board.

The management officers

The secretary and the treasurer at least should have a period of election for two years, possibly three, to give plenty of time for them to learn the ropes and to gain some continuity with the local authority.

The management committee

The world of allotments is changing. In the majority of local authorities, the management committee is replacing the old relationship between the council and the allotments committee. The management committee might include local councillors, community police, a church minister – particularly when the land belongs to the church – a local education authority representative, which may or may not include the LEA allotments officer.

The purpose of this committee is to oversee the general progress of the allotments, deal with wider issues such as fencing, crime, disputes with residents and appeals about rates, charges and access issues. These management groups often have a range of expertise and contacts and their support can be useful, especially when it comes to making applications for local grants, sometimes known as 'cash grants'.

HOW TO PREPARE FOR THE MANAGEMENT MEETING

Usually two or three committee members are invited to the meeting, normally chaired by the secretary of the allotments. Such meetings can be monthly or bi-monthly, depending on the workload of the site.

- **Taking minutes** This is an important job. The minutes should be available for all to see and should be used by all the committee members to communicate with the plot-holders.

  The minute-taker should not be the secretary or treasurer, but another officer. The points of minuting should be clarified at the time of writing down. The phrase 'What should I minute for that?' is the way to be sure the minutes will be accurate.
- **Agenda** The agenda should be sent to all those attending the meeting. You don't need every officer at the meeting – draw up a rota of attendees who get to one meeting in three unless there is something urgent, or unless it is specifically requested that such a person attends.
- **Passing of the minutes** The agenda always starts with the passing of the minutes, when the previous meeting's minutes are read out. The members vote on whether they agree the minutes were a true and accurate record, or discuss changes.
- **Matters arising** from the minutes provides an opportunity for members to report on progress.
- **Points for discussion** The agenda then continues to list the points for discussion. These points might come from the plot-holders, and it is hoped that communication between committee members and plot-holders will be free and comfortable.
- **Any other business** usually ends the agenda, though this can go on for some time. It provides an opportunity for people to bring things up and get them minuted for action next time.

Maintenance – what's what

Drainage

You can often see where the drainage is poor, but there are other indicators to be dealt with. For example, does one area of the site have more onion rot than others? Often this is an indication of poor drainage, so the committee should watch (or listen) out for complaints from gardeners. Remedial drainage work is important and should be ongoing, especially as the land changes over time.

Maintaining sheds and greenhouses is an important part of keeping the site safe, especially if there are children around.

Sunken paths

When gardeners add large amounts of manure or compost, the level of their plot rises. An inch a year is not uncommon, and this has implications for paths between plots. Plots never grow uniformly, and consequently paths become twisted and difficult to use. Helping plot-holders repair paths is important.

Sheds and greenhouses

Many allotments have guidelines outlining where sheds and greenhouses can be sited and the dimensions permitted. It is the role of the maintenance officers to ensure these requirements are adhered to. Buildings cast shadows across plots and may lead to disputes among neighbours. Forcing the size, shape and position of sheds and greenhouses creates a uniformity and causes shadows to be cast on each other's sheds rather than over the plots.

Polytunnels

Some associations forbid polytunnels, others welcome them. The provision of a community polytunnel is an excellent way to help gardeners start their crops, and may cost less than you think. A well-built tunnel, in the centre of the allotments, provides communal space, is easier to protect from outside influences (stones and balls) and makes a good brew stop or rain shelter in winter.

Toilets

It might not be an easy thing to care for, but a toilet is a boon for allotments. You may be lucky enough to have a dedicated building or clubhouse with toilet facilities. The minimum you need is a good Portaloo, regularly cleaned, and the addition of some flowers and handwash.

Money is generally available from the Big Lottery Fund to build toilet blocks (*see Funding for allotments, page 26*). You can do most of the work yourselves to build a toilet block. There is bound to be a bricklayer, chippie, plumber and plasterer on your site (or someone else's site) and you can dig the land drain, but you will need a contractor to connect the water supply from the mains and the drains to the sewer. Planning permission may need to be obtained

A COMPOSTING TOILET

If plumbing is a problem you could always install a composting toilet. There are a variety of building methods – have a search online. The simplest type consists of a bucket, a piece of drainage tube that vents to the top of the bucket, some dry soaking material and a lid. Preferably the lid has a seat built into it.

Do not use the compost to grow vegetables. After a year, the material can be dug out and used to grow roses or other non-food items.

Community areas

The provision of a nature walk enables schoolchildren and others to visit the site, and at the same time allows local wildlife to flourish. Raised beds for disabled gardeners are another project your paths and fences committee can get involved in. In particular, raised beds made from concrete fencing so wheelchair access is feasible will attract grants. Such beds are not the sole realm of disabled gardeners, but can also be offered to prospective plot-holders on waiting lists to ease them into allotments society.

The gate

In my opinion, this is the only place where the committee should be prescriptive and firm when it comes to rules. Keeping gates closed and locked, especially if you have vandalism problems, is a must. In particular, safety issues when there are vulnerable people on the plot, need to be pressed home – *lock the gate*.

Some societies have a buddy system to ensure there is always someone on the plot at any one time (within reason) so if members feel the need for support, it is at hand.

It doesn't follow that, because the gate is locked you have to be unwelcoming. A good, friendly sign giving instructions as to when access can be had is a great thing. A bell placed by the gate to ring when there is someone on site, and removed when there is no one at home, works quite well.

A homemade toilet, paid for with grants. The society had to dig and lay the drain, but the waterboard had to connect to the soil main.

The most important rule on the plot is to lock the gate!

Funding for allotments

All kinds of funding is available for allotments, both local and national. Unfortunately, the names and origins of the grants are subject to change, but we hope we can offer enough information to help you start your fund-raising journey.

An important starting point is to be able to prove that you need cash for a project and to quantify how the money will help the association and the wider population or environment. This will be made easier if your site has a publicity officer, plenty of communication material, produces a newsletter and has a presence *(see Publicity and newsletter secretaries, page 20, and Keep in touch, page 15)*. This way you will be able to reach potential users and potential beneficiaries and have their support when it comes to applying for funds.

For example, if you want to buy land, fencing materials or plants for a wildlife area, it will be helpful to have your local school on board which might want to make use of the space from time to time.

Local grants

A number of grants are available from the local authorities, even in difficult financial times. Often called cash grants, each ward has an allocation of funds for local groups. They are usually for capital projects where there is a physical outcome, such as a toilet, a path, a gate or a clubhouse, and normally they are about £2,000 in value.

In your area these grants might have another name and involve different kinds of bidding. One bidding I was involved with included a presentation night where all the applicants for funds came together in a church hall. The various applicant groups dressed in costumes that illustrated their request. Other bidding rounds are just paperwork affairs.

To apply for such awards, start with your local councillor, who will be able to furnish you with all the necessary information. Some local authorities employ liaison officers for each ward, and a telephone call to the Town Hall is your first point of access.

Matched funding

Sometimes you will be asked to match grants, which means the council will give you money for projects so long as you meet half the costs. It does not matter how you make up the sum – you can raise the money yourselves, you can ask a benefactor, a government or council source, or approach the private sector. The purpose of this is to ensure you another examination to check the viability of your proposal, and some wider financial checks and balances.

Allotment-wide finances

Each year the local authority sets a budget for spending on allotments. Sometimes this can be a small amount and funds are difficult to come by. However, there is nothing stopping you from negotiating a rent rebate to go towards repairs and projects, which in itself is like a grant.

There may be other ways of achieving what you need. For example, if you want to raise money for a toilet, there may well be a number of Portacabins no longer in use belonging to the council. Being part of the local authority-wide allotments' group and making known your needs is a good idea, as is talking to your allotments officer or local councillor.

Call for help

It is amazing how a call for help can create funding in kind. This is where the value of good community relations pays off. A few well-made cards in shops, or notices on any of your web pages or in the local press, will provide a wealth of responses. One group I know got paving stones and concrete fencing enough to make disabled raised beds for free and fitted them, too. This was in return for a photograph and an article in the local paper. The company donating spent about £200 in materials and its own time, and achieved hundreds of pounds-worth of free publicity in the process. The local newspaper covered the story and it went on its website, too.

Water companies may provide a successful route into gaining grants. Most water companies have an ethics or ethical community or community relations department that may have both access to funds and knowledge of other organisations that are giving away cash to allotments.

Non-local authority grants

Big Lottery Fund
tel 0845 4102030
www.biglotteryfund.org.uk

The Big Lottery Fund has lots of money to give away and is divided into regions. All the information is on the website or you can call the number. There are a number of initiatives which target various groups, such as villages, young people, the elderly and people with disabilities. So if you have plans for raised beds, for example, or access issues, or a toilet, this would be a good place to start.

The Co-operative

tel 0161 8275879
e-mail customer.relations@co-op.co.uk

The Co-operative gives grants of differing sizes, and you stand a chance if your allotments are close to one of its shops. It has different emphases in various areas. Fighting crime and improving health are included in its remit, so if you need to build a fence or you want to help people grow food, you are in with a shout.

Allotments Regeneration Initiative

www.farmgarden.org.uk/ari/grants

This new venture works with anyone seeking to keep an allotment going, or starting a new set of allotments. Its website is packed with information and some of it refers to grants. For instance, it offers a small bursary for travelling – it is a great idea to visit other sites for inspiration. It also has informative ideas about community groups, which is worthwhile reading when applying for grants.

The National Society for Allotment and Leisure Gardeners

tel 01536 266576
www.nsalg.org.uk

The National Society for Allotment and Leisure Gardeners (NSALG) has a page dedicated to allotment funding on its website. It is not comprehensive, but there are some sources you might consider. You can always contact the society via its website and talk to one of its officers.

Community polytunnel purchased with Lottery Fund money.

Disabled access beds bought with Lottery Funding.

How to run a tool share

Setting the rules

Whoever runs the tool shed has an important job on the allotment *(see Tools secretary, page 22)*. The tools can share space with the stores at a pinch, especially if room is at a premium. However, tools should be kept out of view of non-gardening members and other visitors and should never go off-site. Ideally, the tools should be housed where only gardening members can find them, so people are not put under pressure by having to say 'no' to members of the public.

Laying down the law

Everyone who borrows tools from the store must understand the terms of use, otherwise the tools secretary's job will be a nightmare. Having to chase tools, or clean them, or even repair them is not on.

- Plot-holders should mark down in a book when they take a tool, or ask the tools secretary to book them out a tool.
- The tool should be returned clean – no mud attached to the rotors, wheels, blades, and no grass on the cutters.

Always make sure the tool shed is well organised.

THE TOOL-STORE BUDGET

A budget should be available to cover both the maintenance of tools in the store and the purchase of new ones. The majority of tool shares on allotments exist because the tools have been given by plot-holders, and that is fine except new people trying an allotment for the first time will not do very well with poor quality, cast-off equipment.

The maintenance of power tools should always be done professionally. The receipts should be kept to show that you have done all you need to keep the machine in good order in case someone complains or through misuse has either an accident or breaks something.

- Any petrol should be paid for, rather than replaced, that way you are sure to have an uncontaminated supply – trying to run a two-stroke Rotavator on diesel is a real pain.
- Some tools, especially power tools, should not be used by anyone who has not been shown the safe way to operate them.
- Although the tools secretary has an obligation to keep the tools well-serviced, it should be made clear to plot-holders that they borrow them at their own risk.

Having friends to help with your plot turns hard work into a joy.

Organising a work day

The tool store and the people associated with it have much to contribute to work days. Many allotments have a programme of work that needs to be done during the year, such as making paths or installing buildings. Also, it is a good idea if you can, from time to time or as required, help new allotmenteers, or people having difficulties with their plot for one reason or another.

My first plot was a junk yard, filled with all kinds of rubbish, tyres, old sheds, bicycle frames, oil, an old chicken run and so on. It would have taken me years to clear it, and a small fortune too, were it not for the help of my fellow plot-holders who spent Saturday mornings on my plot for months, helping me get it straight. The events were a great chance to get to know people, and we had brews and BBQs as well as making my plot into one of the best there was.

The identification of jobs and the general whip-round to get them done

■ means that not everything is done by just a few
■ promotes an enjoyable ethos, a fun place to be

WHAT YOU SHOULD NOT ATTEMPT TO DO

Unless you have the skills (and qualifications) and the appropriate permissions there are a number of jobs you should not attempt. For instance, you should insist the council does the following:

■ laying outside pavements and fences, road tracks and official signage
■ connecting anything to the mains electricity, gas, and drains
■ building brick walls about 1m (3ft) high
■ erecting towers, including water towers or for wind turbine electricity generating.

■ encourages people to attend to their plots regularly
■ allows people to learn various gardening techniques.

Organising a show

This is a year-long task that starts as soon as last year's show ends *(see Show secretary, page 20)*. The preparations for the show include finding a venue that has sufficient tables for all the categories you have prizes for. You might have access to a venue for free, or you may have to pay. There is plenty of scope for sponsorship to cover all the aspects of the show, as your major selling point is the schedule, and the opportunity to mention sponsors at the show and in the local newspaper.

The various categories can be individually sponsored, and the newspaper will welcome the idea of a couple of free pages, so you can sell the idea of sponsors' names being mentioned in the paper.

If you can show pictures of the previous year's event and a company's promotional images from that show, you will easily be able to pull in sponsors. Often it is as simple as walking down the high street.

Choose the right crop a week before the show. They will be perfect when you pick them on the morning of the show.

The schedule

This is the most important part of the show because it points out how the individual sections will be judged. You have to tie down exactly what people are to exhibit, and how they qualify to enter each section.

■ List the committee members of the show, and of the allotments site if necessary.

■ Thank everyone for last year's efforts, mention winners and sponsors.

■ Include the entry form for next year's show. You should not accept entries except by this form, and the form should be unmodified.

■ Outline prize money and awards, so entrants know what they could win.

■ Mention when winners are going to have to return their cups and silverware before the show, and explain the arrangements for engraving and so on.

Rules

The list of rules should include:

■ Entry fees

■ Arrangements for setting up

■ How entries are to be presented

■ Entrants should bring their own plates, etc

■ The judges' decisions will be final, and that means final

■ Neither the committee nor anyone else will be responsible for breakages

■ When participants can collect their entries and awards

■ Entrants should be asked to sign a declaration on the form stating that what they are entering is their own work; they have not entered anything unfairly (best wine from the supermarket in the wine classes, for example); they qualify for certain sections (no adults in the children's classes).

Classes

The outlined classes are then displayed on the schedule for people to choose, for example:

■ **Open Classes** (adult and/or child)

■ **Class 12** Plate of 3 identical potatoes, any one named variety, white

■ **Class 13** Plate of 3 identical potatoes, any one named variety, red.

These classes show exactly what is needed: a plate, 3 potatoes – as identical as possible – and a label that tells the judge the name of the variety. The rest is up to the judge.

There could be as many as 200 categories (or more) for people to enter and during judging no one else is normally allowed in the show area. This is a great reason for combining the event with an open day, to give everyone a chance to do something.

Organising an open day

The idea of an open day is to introduce the local community to the allotments. Many allotment societies abhor the idea of having the public on the site, and you can understand it when they are under siege, or finding it difficult because of vandalism, but some allotments do open and are happily situated to bring people into the site and show off a little.

You need to have some reason for bringing people in. Of course there are the plots to wander around, but this is not always the main draw. A Good Life Day, where you show visitors how an allotment can change the way they live, is another matter. Think about the expertise you have in the society and perhaps try putting on a gardener's question time or a plant hospital.

Sometimes you have to be imaginative about getting people through the doors. A local school link is often a great resource. For example, inviting a school band to play will bring the parents along too. Publicising your community plot and offering parent-and-child gardening can also attract a number of people hoping for an allotment.

Use the shop
There is nothing to stop the society from marketing its shop and gaining non-gardening members. Make announcements, such as: 'We are now stocking eggs so come and have a look around our open day!'

Food and drinks
To be honest, it is much better to get someone else to do the catering for an open day. You could have an ice-cream van or a professional hog roast, almost anything other than doing it yourself. This way you can be sure to be within the public health regulations.

Advertising
Schools, shop windows, the allotment gates, the allotment newsletter, the church newsletter and the local newspaper are brilliant for getting the message out. Local radio is a very

Getting involved with your community can pay dividends.

A scarecrow competition can benefit everyone on the allotment.

effective way of reaching people – most of the BBC local radio stations have a morning programme that allows community groups to announce their events.

Allotment newsletter
It might seem a little odd, but just because you are planning an open day does not mean that all the plot-holders will know about it. Some never get as far as the clubhouse notice board, and an allotment newsletter, hopefully delivered by hand, with a chat, will make sure everyone hears about it. This way you are more likely to get their family and friends to come along too.

Local residents
If you are in a position to deliver flyers to your nearest housing, you are in a great position to advertise your event, and encourage a local following for your society. Many allotment societies have regular social events, some even have a bar or dance, providing a chance to give your open day a plug.

Use the Internet
Someone on the site will be Internet savvy. There is a huge allotment representation on the Internet, with societies using Facebook and Twitter where you can attract a following that interacts daily, and where you can post all kinds of messages, events and get immediate responses.

PLANNING YOUR PLOT

A well-planned plot not only looks good, it is also easier to work.

Getting a new plot can be confusing. All that land, all those weeds! The first thing you should consider is how you imagine your plot developing over time, and how you will get there. Remember, it is not a sprint, this allotment gardening, it is a marathon. So don't become downcast by the enormity of the task – get a plan and stick to it.

The four essentials

There are a number of important points to remember: you need light, water and good soil. Then there are neighbours.

1 Light
Light is important because plants will not grow without it. If your plot runs north–south it will be fully illuminated throughout the day, but if it runs east–west, it will be prone to shadows and be more likely to have cold spots. Look out for shadows and how they might cross the plot, and if there is anything you should do about it.

2 Water
Without water, nothing lives. If you have lots of weeds, you can be sure there is a reasonable amount of water in the soil. The presence of sedges, in particular, suggests that water is quite deep and you will have a good plot. If there is a lot of moss, it might indicate a soil that does not drain too well.

Clay soil is cold and has so much water that oxygen does not get to the roots of plants. But at least there is water, and

Familiarise yourself with the rules about water on the site and plan to collect rainwater.

Test the soil for drainage above all else. You can increase fertility and change the pH easily, but increasing drainage can be hard work.

over time you will be able to do something about the structure.

Locate the mains tap and find out about watering restrictions. Some allotments forbid any form of hosepipe watering, even in times of plenty. Collect rainwater, which is more natural and is not filled with chemicals to make it safe to drink, but be aware that rainwater can be poisonous to some delicate plants. Be sure to keep it safely – water butts should always have a lid on them, preferably with a lock if possible.

3 Soil
Look at the height of the soil in relation to paths and other plots. It may well be higher as a result of constantly adding fertiliser, a sure sign of a well-worked plot. Weeds mean the plot supports plant life, so this is not as bad as it might at first appear, but there are some tests you can do to find out more.

Colour The darker the soil, the more organic matter there is within it. Throw a handful in a bucket of water and leave it for a day. Particles floating at the surface show there to be organic matter in the soil.

Water content Take another handful and squeeze it into a ball. If it sticks together and just begins to break apart, there is the perfect amount of water. Moulded into a ball that stays put, or even drips, and you will need to think about drainage.

pH test I rarely test for pH because I know from the amount of lime I have added to the soil that it is either neutral or slightly alkaline.

4 Neighbours
Neighbours will let you know how their plot has developed, what is and is not allowed and what the general problems are on the allotments. You do not need to slavishly follow what they advise, but clearly a new plot-holder will be a source of interest to existing ones.

Looking is a part of planning. Keep your eyes open and take your time to plan your plot.

Mark out your cleared plot and stick to your design.

Layout

Draw out a plan for the whole plot, even if you are not going to implement it all at once. You probably won't be able to prepare the entire plot without calling on an army of volunteers.

Paths and buildings

Bearing in mind local regulations about buildings, greenhouses and polytunnels, plan where these are going to go and set the paths in place. Mark out the various beds and structures. If the plot is overgrown, cut out the worst of the growth and burn or compost the material, then cover the area with a ground covering fabric. This will allow you to uncover sections of the allotment and work on it by degrees, knowing there will be no more weeds to deal with, and that the areas covered the longest will remain weed free until you get to them.

Remember that covering the soil to reduce weeds is by no means 100% effective. Once disturbed by digging, an army of weed seeds will be ready to burst into life, and you will need to spend a long time with the hoe clearing them.

Beds

There is an ongoing debate about whether beds should be raised or not. The fundamental idea of raised beds is simple: you have a discrete area in which to grow and you can keep off the soil contained within. Raised beds are expensive, but once constructed they are easily maintained. You can also incorporate coverings, polytunnel-like plastics and horticultural fleece.

On the other hand, there is some wastage of soil, and you are restricted when it comes to the use of Rotavators and other equipment. You are also hampered if you wish to change the layout of your plot at a later date.

Crop rotation

Crop rotation means not growing the same crop on the same ground in successive years. There are two distinct reasons for doing this: disease and fertility.

Crops take different amounts of nutrients from the soil and also attract all kinds of pests. If you grow crops in the same bed year-on-year you will encourage pest problems.

Before we look at crop rotation on allotments it is worth noting that we rarely rotate crops for fertility. Many gardeners, and a lot of articles in books and magazines, wrongly superimpose ideas and methods that are suited to agriculture rather than horticulture. Rotation for fertility does not work in the same way on an allotment as it does on a 30-acre field. It is one thing rotating a set of fields a few acres in size – that works well. But doing the same in a garden that is only a 20th of an acre is something completely different.

However, rotation to keep disease at bay, or reduce it, certainly is important on the allotment.

Using raised beds can help with rotation by marking exactly where you grow.

Fertility levels

The average dose for manure in an organic system is 4 tonnes per 0.4 hectare (3.9 tons per acre). This means that the average allotment should receive about 200kg (440lb, about 20 barrow-loads) of well-rotted manure. The average allotment gets around three times more fertiliser per square metre (square yard) than the average field. Not just manure, but compost and concentrates, too.

Over the years the fertility of the soil can build up to very high levels and some plants, such as spinach, accumulate nitrates in their leaves, sometimes to unhealthy levels. Also, crops like carrots do not like much fertility as it makes them split. It is always a good idea to have at least one unfertilised area in a rotation system to reduce the fertility.

A rotation system in which one section is fertilised heavily for crops such as potatoes, then the following year this is followed by beans, then a fertiliser-free year of salads, will prevent the soil from building up too much fertility.

This sounds almost the opposite to what is natural, but the evidence is there. Look at an old allotment where the layers of manure added each year will have brought the soil level way over the paths.

A four-year rotation

Some beds are going to be fairly permanent – rhubarb, strawberries and asparagus, for instance. Some gardeners have permanent areas for green manure, such as comfrey

and borage, and still more have permanent herb beds. Areas for flowers and biodiversity take up more room and if you have a pond for slug-eating frogs, it is a good idea to keep this well away from the rotating parts of your allotment.

Other areas, such as for salads, squashes and artichokes, can be rotated separately, and these also fill in to other parts of the plot, as can garlic and herbs.

The rest of the plot can be laid out as four beds (flat or raised) where the major crops will rotate:

- Potatoes
- Peas and beans
- Cabbages, swedes, sprouts
- Onions, sweet corn, carrots, turnips (some people separate root crops from onions).

The plot to receive potatoes is always manured when the final crops are removed, and then the ground is limed before planting brassicas. You can add compost after the peas and beans if you like, and additional lime after the potatoes.

This system allows for three years before you have to think about putting a crop where it was before, and gives two years for the pH to reduce after liming so you can grow potatoes without them developing scab.

Well-rotted muck

On one allotment I had for many years we used to get manure from the abattoir. It made me sad to think of those animals, but as you can imagine the abattoir had a lot of manure to shift so it was cheap. We found that unless it was

really well-rotted it was full of seeds and consequently the potato patch would be full of weeds.

You have to get your muck hot to kill the seeds, and just leaving it open to the rain is not good enough. Get the pile warm by covering it to insulate the heap, and in this way the temperature will build up. More importantly, the heat will kill many of the fungal spores in the manure, making it better for applying to the soil.

Dealing with disease

Understandably, if you grow crops in the same soil, year after year, it will accumulate pests for that crop and you will see yields reduce regardless of how much fertiliser you give the plants.

I once knew a man who grew onions on the same block year-on-year, and it did work for him because each year he had a huge bonfire where he planted the onions. The fire sterilised the soil and eliminated the pests. Generally, you need to be sure the common pests for a particular crop can die back before that crop is replanted on that piece of land.

Potatoes prefer neutral soils and get all scabby in lime. (You can still eat scabby potatoes, but probably would prefer not to.) The current process of growing cabbages in high concentrations of lime is counter-productive for potatoes, so put as long a time between the crops.

Another disease problem on all allotments is clubroot, which affects cabbages in particular. It is carried by a fungus, *Plasmodiophora brassicae*, and is common among all the members of the *Cruciferae* family, including brassicas (cabbages, cauliflowers, sprouts and so on). It is passed around on people's boots and causes the roots to distort and become useless. The problem with small plots is that when you walk on the soil you spread spores all over your land. This is an excellent reason for installing raised beds that are no more than just over 1m (4ft) wide. This way you can reach to the centre without touching the soil at all.

There was once a chemical treatment, but it has now been removed from sale. I have seen one or two plots where a mat soaked in Jeyes' fluid served to disinfect everyone's feet before entering the plot.

Rotation and trenches

The usual way of making a bean trench is to dig a trench that is more or less one-and-a-half spades deep and then fill the bottom third with kitchen waste. This is then covered with soil and the beans are transplanted into it.

To be honest, these trenches have been used for generations and some of my old books swear by them (assuming they swore at all in those days). However, these days I am troubled by the idea of planting crops into still-rotting material, especially if the material has come out of the garden. Disease can spread easily, and the rotting process hardly makes this better.

It is probably better to use really well-rotted manure or compost, or a combination of the two in trenches. If you are relying on the trench to create heat for the soil, use some plastic.

TOP TIP

BEAN BED BENEFIT

Try to alter the position of the bean bed each year and you will find the soil in the old bed is brilliant for carrots and turnips, not so high in nutrients, but good enough.

Runner beans growing happily in a trench.

TOP TIP

INTRODUCE FLOWERS

Why not put some flowers into your rotation? You will have to dig them up before you re-crop, but a bed of annuals makes a really lovely display and is doing the soil good at the same time.

Grass paths are hard work – you have to mow and edge them – but they look good when you set them.

Paths

You can easily tell a good allotments site – the people are welcoming and can be seen drinking tea nearly all the time. In the clubhouse there are cakes and cold drinks in the fridge, and the paths are all straight.

It can be hard work keeping up the paths and many societies have a rota of gangs, almost enforced labour, for repairing and making paths. Some ask individual plot-holders to take responsibility for their path and the main path at the end or edge of the plot.

Car parking

If possible, the site should have a car park to avoid having cars parked all over the larger paths. That is not to say you cannot drive to your plot, but you will have to return the car to the car park once unloaded.

If your site does not have a car park, consider converting a plot. Provision of a car park does not have to be expensive, nor hard work, and the delivery of a few tonnes of aggregate topped with gravel is usually enough. It looks better if edged with shuttering rather than allowing the gravel to spill off at the ends of the car parking area. Most sites have a car park near the clubhouse.

If you use paving to edge a path, make sure it is buried properly – better to use some other material. Don't use bricks, you get lots of snails in them.

Major routes

These are the larger paths that need to be set in place for motorised access around the site and are best metalled. Ideally, they should be created by contractors, and you may be able to get financial assistance from the local authority. You will also need permission from the council.

Smaller paths

One of the problems with good allotment plots is the soil level rises over the years, as year on year the gardener adds well-rotted manure in order to grow potatoes. The edges of the plot collapse onto the paths, which disappear under the weight of new soil.

There are a number of ways of dealing with this problem. Some allotments ask plot-holders to maintain a side bed around the perimeter, which can be as little as six inches across – often planted with flowers, carrots or salads – inside which are they allowed to add compost or manure and thus paths are preserved.

Raised beds are another solution.

Path size

The paths mark the boundaries and should be wide enough to take a person pushing a wheelbarrow. When the wheelbarrow is set down there should be enough space for the back legs to rest within the path, and ideally there should be enough room to get round the barrow without having to climb over it.

Laying stones has the benefit of making a noise, deterring intruders, but they are difficult to push a wheelbarrow on.

These concrete slabs were set professionally, along with the concrete raised beds for disabled access. Note the gaps between the beds are set for wheelchair access.

TOP TIP

SETTING A PATH

Another way of setting paving stones is to lay on a mixture of sand and cement (4:1), which will set hard once the stones have been watered in.

Or you can try laying paving on gravel with five blobs of cement to set the stone hard. Either way you have to brush in a sand and cement mixture between the stones.

Laying a concrete paving path

You will need:
- Sand
- Heavy mallet
- Spade
- Shuttering of preserved wood
- Builder's level
- Paving slabs.

The path should be level and the slabs butted carefully so there are no steps between them. It is more expensive, but allows more space, to have the slabs laid wide rather than long-ways.

1 Assuming this is a new path, take off the grass, or other vegetation, and lay it on a compost heap, upside down. Dig the path at least 10cm (4in) deep and level it as best you can. It does not have to be perfectly level at this stage.

2 Lay treated 100 x 50 (4 x 2; 100 x 25/4 x 1 will do) wood along the edge of the path, so there is enough space for the paving stones to fit snuggly. This is called shuttering, and has to be level. It will help to make the path last a long time.

3 Hold the shuttering in place with stakes driven into the path area on one side and the earth of the cut-out soil on the other. It is important the shuttering is held securely.

4 Half-fill the path with dry sand and firm well. Lay the stones on this so they are level with the shuttering, using a heavy rubber mallet to bring the tops of the paving level and in line with the shuttering.

5 Once the paving is in place, scatter sand on the stones and brush into the cracks.

6 Keep off the path for a few days and then look out for the paving stones settling at an angle and adjust.

Laying a bark path

This is a good path and is far less work than a paved structure, but in the end is possibly higher maintenance. It is still preferable to dig out and lay sand for this path.

You will need:
- Spade
- Shuttering of preserved wood (100 x 50/4 x 2 is best here)
- Sand
- Horticultural weed suppressant sheeting
- Bark chips.

Dig out the path as for the paved path *(see above)*, and lay sand between the levelled shuttering as before. Cover the sand with a number of layers of horticultural ground cover, with the edges well tucked into the sand next to the shuttering, or tack the ground cover to the shuttering in a loose fashion. Fill the space with bark chips.

This kind of path will need weed killer (or hand weeding) every year and replenishing with fresh bark. It makes a soft path that is quite durable, though harder to wheel a barrow over than a paved one.

Using bark as a path filler is good, but high maintenance.

Fences between plots should not cast shadows -
this wire fence is fine

Fences

About 50% of all the allotments I have visited allow fences between plots. It comes as quite a shock when you visit an allotment with a large fence regime. One wonders what the need is for a 1.2m (4ft) high fence between neighbouring allotments, you would have thought they would spoil the light.

Perimeter fencing
The perimeter fence and gates are the local authority's responsibility and should be erected and maintained by the authority. If your outer fencing is in disrepair, and is not up to keeping out intruders, then the council should be dealing with it.

As a committee, do not settle for helpful handouts of materials, or drips of cash. The consequences of someone damaging themselves on a half-made fence are important considerations.

Internal fencing
Some allotments have a compound, partly for car parking and partly for sheds and stores. Fencing around compounds should not be too high. It should not tempt an intruder to climb high, nor should it encourage someone to jump from a fence to a roof. Keeping it low is the best idea.

Building a wire post fence

This is hard work, it will make you sweat on a cold day.
There are two ways of doing it.

1 Having lined up the fence, dig holes to receive the posts, approximately 1/3 the length of the post. The post should be made from treated timber. You can fill the hole with concrete, or fix into the earth.

2 This post is only holding chicken wire, so it is knocked home with a heavy hammer.

3 Check the post for vertical all round, so it is not leaning in any direction, then secure the hole with compressed earth.

4 Set the stays in line with the direction of the fence. Corner stays are fixed at 45 degrees. Every other post should be stayed, but if the fence has to take heavy use, all the posts should be reinforced with stays.

5 Use staples, also known as 'U' nails to set the mesh or wire in place.

6 Tension the fence before fixing to the other posts.

Chicken wire should be very secure.

Wire netting

Interlink netting makes an excellent fence and is much easier to erect. You need a full height pole or bracket – often a metallic angle – set in concrete and properly vertical. The fencing is attached to one end and tensioned by wires that run at the top, middle and bottom of the fence. Posts are set at 3m (10ft) intervals. Doors need a proper framework and such a structure makes a good chicken run.

When hedges become fences

I used to have a hedge of blackcurrant bushes that ran the length of the path between me and my neighbour. Pretty soon, he followed suit. The result was that you could not get the wheelbarrow along the path because the bushes spilled over.

If you are going to grow a hedge, plant the bushes 30cm (12in) away from the side of the path. The same goes for espaliered fruit on a wire fence. Remember, you need space to work comfortably all around the fence.

This simple privet hedge makes a good fence, but where does the shade fall? And, how much better would the hedge be if it was full of fruit, berries and nuts to gather?

Water

Water on allotments is one of the scariest things there is. I worry about the safety of children around water butts, ponds and any other freestanding water, and would make a plea that no one ever has water storage without proper lids in place.

Some societies have a blanket hose-pipe ban, meaning people have to water with a can and collect rainwater. However, you are usually allowed to fill the water butt with water through a hose.

Collecting water from a shed

This is the easiest way to collect water. All you need is a gutter and a drainpipe, and in good allotment style, these can be easily made from tins, scrounged or purchased.

For every millimetre of rain, a square metre (square yard) of roof will collect 1 litre (1.8pt) of water. So your average shed roof will collect about 300 litres (66gal) of water, less spillage, evaporation, and so on. This is not a lot of water, but if you collect it from your greenhouse and polytunnel as well, it soon mounts up. Save it for emergency watering – don't forget the plot has also been watered at the same rate as your roof.

You can stack water butts together by cutting a hole at the highest point of the highest butt and feeding this into the next one down and so on until you feed the lowermost butt.

Collecting water on an open site

If you have an open site where no sheds or structures are allowed, the best bet is to collect water from cold frames. I have seen butts with an upturned lid on them, collecting about 90 litres (20gal) of water a year. However, there is usually a mains water supply on site and there is nothing to stop you filling a butt from the tap.

Throw away the rose

I like watering with a rose, but it spreads water about, increases humidity and causes excessive evaporation. If you can, throw away the rose and place strategic pots or cut-off water bottles in the ground into which you can water more effectively, and therefore waste less.

> ## TOP TIP
>
> ### THE SECRET POWER OF THE HOE
>
> A Victorian author of a gardening book said he was able to bring more water up with the hoe rather than the pot. I did not believe it at first, but the idea works, unless there has been a serious drought. If you hoe up the surface soil you will cause water to gently and invisibly replace it by the surface tension of the water drawing water from below. This will also get to your roots.

Collecting run off from taps protects the path and saves water.

Collecting rainwater is an excellent use of free water – make sure it is safe for children by fitting a good lid.

PRACTICAL MATTERS

Take your time when digging. A bad back could stop your gardening altogether.

The art of good gardening is rhythm, something that permeates from the way one digs, plants out, sows seeds, handles plants, takes them from the pot to the earth. Gardening is more than bashing away with a spade, smashing with a hoe, plonking seeds in place, splashing water about – it has a feel, a special movement all of its own. It is something you pick up from other gardeners and something that takes time to develop.

This chapter looks into some of the more important techniques used in the garden, such as digging and composting, and relates them to the world of the allotment. There are lots of different ways of doing some of these tasks but the first thing you need to check is your soil..

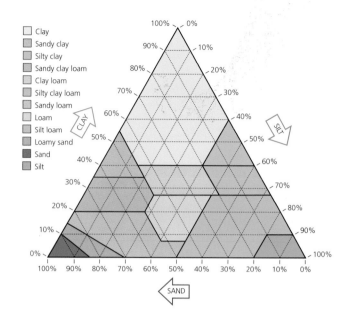

Discovering your soil type

The secret is in the soil

Once you know what type of soil you have, you can avoid crops that are likely to fail. You will also know how to treat your soil to get the best from it year after year.

The diagram shows the range of different common soil types. There are three main types: clay (the most common), sand and silt. A mixture of all three of these in the perfect proportions is called loam.

The type of soil you have also depends on the underlying rock; most overly clay, but chalk is also common. Chalk soils tend to be quite thin and alkaline in nature.

One last soil type, which is less common, but presents its own challenges is peaty soil. Peaty soils are unique in that they are formed by many layers of organic matter that has broken down over many millennia. They are often very acidic and so on their own will only support plants that are adapted to grow in such conditions (see chart, page 51). They often remain very wet in the winter, but can be quite dry in the summer, so need careful management. In these circumstances it is often easier to grow your veg in raised beds using imported loam.

Soil size matters

The relative sizes of the various soil particles can be seen in the diagram and these have a great influence on the properties of the soil; for example, how well it drains, holds on to nutrients and how much air it contains. The mixture of particles of differing sizes is described as the soil's texture.

You can gain some idea of the mixture of particles that make up your soil by half filling a jam jar with soil and then topping up almost to the top with water. Shake the jar for a few seconds and then leave to settle. Large particles such as

stones and sand will sink immediately while tiny particles such as clay may remain in suspension for many days. Organic matter such as little bits of plant waste will float. After a week, look at the layers in the jar to gain some insight into the make-up of your soil. To get a better idea of the type of soil you have, however, follow the steps outlined on the next page.

I know my soil type, what next?

Different soil textures need different management to give their best. They also have advantages and disadvantages, which are handy to know. But before taking spade to plot you need to discover your soil's structure.

What is soil structure?

The structure of a soil simply describes the network of channels, pores and spaces within it, created as the particles clump together (rather than the percentage of particles themselves). Different soils have different structures depending on the percentage of clay, silt or sand they contain. This percentage also determines how easily the structure can be damaged when cultivated.

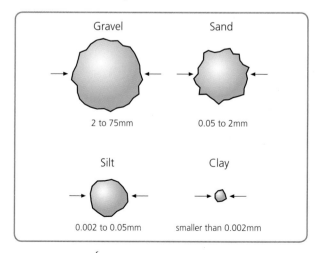

What soil do I have? A step-by-step guide

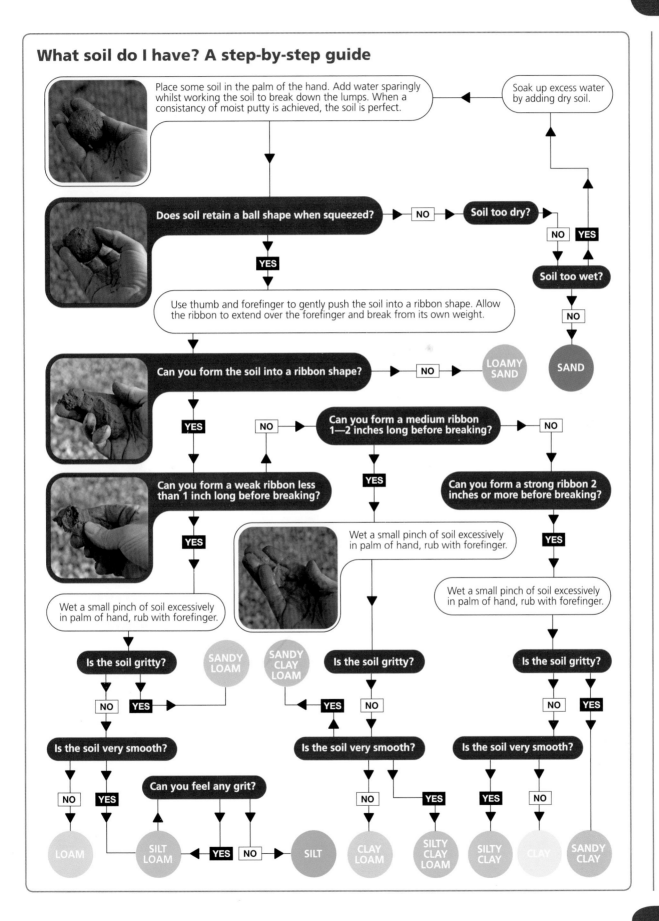

Place some soil in the palm of the hand. Add water sparingly whilst working the soil to break down the lumps. When a consistancy of moist putty is achieved, the soil is perfect.

Soak up excess water by adding dry soil.

Does soil retain a ball shape when squeezed? → NO → **Soil too dry?** → NO / YES

YES ↓

→ **Soil too wet?** → NO

Use thumb and forefinger to gently push the soil into a ribbon shape. Allow the ribbon to extend over the forefinger and break from its own weight.

Can you form the soil into a ribbon shape? → NO → **LOAMY SAND** / **SAND**

YES ↓ | NO → **Can you form a medium ribbon 1—2 inches long before breaking?** → NO

Can you form a weak ribbon less than 1 inch long before breaking? | YES ↓ | **Can you form a strong ribbon 2 inches or more before breaking?**

YES ↓ | → **YES**

Wet a small pinch of soil excessively in palm of hand, rub with forefinger.

Wet a small pinch of soil excessively in palm of hand, rub with forefinger.

Wet a small pinch of soil excessively in palm of hand, rub with forefinger.

Is the soil gritty? — NO / YES → **SANDY LOAM** | **SANDY CLAY LOAM** ← YES — **Is the soil gritty?** — NO | **Is the soil gritty?** — NO / YES

Is the soil very smooth? — NO / YES | **Is the soil very smooth?** — NO / YES | **Is the soil very smooth?** — YES / NO

Can you feel any grit? — YES / NO

LOAM | **SILT LOAM** ← YES / NO → **SILT** | **CLAY LOAM** | **SILTY CLAY LOAM** | **SILTY CLAY** | **CLAY** | **SANDY CLAY**

Soil improving and pH

The essential ingredient

Vegetables are not fussy and will grow well in most soils, but it is important to build and maintain a good crumb structure, as in a loam, since this allows plenty of air to get to the roots while encouraging drainage.

A 'magic' ingredient called humus is what you need to improve poor soils and maintain good ones. It is present in all well-rotted organic matter, including animal manure and plant waste, or compost. Put very simply, humus is a jelly-like substance that is released when anything of organic origin rots. It feeds the soil flora and fauna, helps to hold water and nutrients and in combination with soil microbes which release sticky gums, binds the soil particles of all soil types together, encouraging them to form crumbs. It also darkens the soil, helping it to absorb the sun's rays so warming up faster in spring.

By adding humus in the form of well-rotted compost or manure every autumn and again when planting or as a mulch, it will gradually improve and maintain the structure and fertility of your soil and constitutes the most important job you will do each year in your allotment.

Soil pH

All soils have a natural acidity or alkalinity depending on the parent materials from which they are made, the amount of organic matter they contain (organic matter tends to be acidic), mineral content and, above all, the amount of lime present in the soil. When you measure soil pH, you are really measuring the pH of the water it contains, complete with these dissolved materials.

The acidity or alkalinity of a soil is expressed as its pH on a scale from 0–14 with 0 being very acid (the level of

How does your soil measure up?

SANDY SOIL
Structure Coarse with large air spaces.
Pros Free draining, good aeration, warms quickly and can be worked earlier in the spring.
Cons Poor water and nutrient-holding properties so plants may starve. The structure is easily damaged when cultivating.

CLAY SOIL
Structure Tiny particles with tiny air spaces.
Pros Very fertile since the particles hold on to water and nutrients well.
Cons Remains wet and cold in spring, cracks during dry weather and becomes very hard. It is heavy to work and easily damaged if compacted, and it smears and forms hard pans (impermeable barriers) below the surface if cultivated with a rotary cultivator.

SILTY SOIL
Structure Fine with small air spaces and poor natural aeration. The fragile crumbs break down easily.
Pros Fertile and holds water and nutrients well. Faster than clay to warm in spring.
Cons Forms a crust on the surface during dry weather and puddles in wet weather. Easily damaged by over-cultivating.

LOAMY SOIL
Structure Lots of crumbs which stay together and drain freely, with plenty of air spaces.
Pros Fertile, good water and nutrient holding properties, good aeration. Slower to warm in the spring than sand, but better than clay.
Cons None.

Well drained soils such as this sand are ideal for certain crops, such as asparagus.

Well rotted organic matter such as garden compost contains humus – nature's own soil improver.

hydrochloric acid) and 14 very alkaline (household bleach is 12.5). A pH of 7 is neutral.

In practice, few soils fall lower than 3 or higher than 9. Plants grow best when they are in a soil that offers their preferred level of acidity or alkalinity and most are happy in a slightly acid soil, pH 6.5. This is less critical than is often suggested since most plants – vegetables included – can grow in a wide range of soil pH, certainly from 6–7.5 (*see alongside*). Much above or below this and the pH starts to affect the availablity of the nutrients in the soil and may lead to nutrient deficiencies.

Testing and adjusting soil pH

Testing the soil to check its pH level is easy since all you need is a simple test kit available from your local garden centre. Place a representative sample of soil into the test tube or test pot supplied, add the reagent supplied and some distilled water and check the colour against a chart or coloured scale on the test pot.

The kit will also come with advice as to how much lime you may need to add to lift the pH to the required level. Most of us will need to raise pH rather than lower it, since rainfall and the addition of fertilisers and organic matter tend to have an acidifying effect on the soil. This is usually done by adding garden lime (ground limestone or chalk), which is the safest way of providing this nutrient. Lime can be applied once a year if a test proves it necessary, having taken account of your planned crop rotation.

Soils can be made more acidic, for example on areas overlying chalk, by adding sulphur chips. In extreme cases it is often easier to grow crops in a raised bed using imported soil rather than try to adjust the existing material.

pH preferences of some commonly grown vegetables	
Asparagus	6.5–7.5
Beans, climbing	6.5–7.5
Beets	6.0–7.5
Broccoli	6.0–7.0
Brussels sprouts	6.0–7.5
Cabbages	6.0–7.5
Carrots	5.5–7.0
Cauliflowers	5.5–7.5
Celery	6.5–7.5
Cucumbers	5.5–7.0
Garlic	5.5–8.0
Kale	6.0–7.5
Lettuces	6.5–7.5
Onions/garlic	5.5–8.0
Peas	5.5–7.0
Peppers	5.5–7.0
Potatoes	5.0–6.0
Pumpkins	5.5–7.5
Radishes	6.0–7.0
Spinach	6.0–7.5
Squash, crookneck	5.5–7.0
Squash, Hubbard	5.5–7.0
Tomatoes	5.5–7.5

Our pH test gave a result of pH 6.5 or slightly acid – a good level for most vegetables.

TOP TIP

WHEN TO LIME

Never add lime and fertilisers together. They react when mixed, and the lime 'locks up' some of the nutrients, while making others too readily available.

Instead, plan which veg will be grown on which areas of the plot (your crop rotation plan), then lime areas where brassica crops are to be planted, since they like a more alkaline soil. Lime also deters clubroot, a damaging disease in these crops.

Do not add lime to a bed intended for potatoes, since this encourages another disease called potato scab. Give this bed a dressing of organic matter. (*See Crop rotation, page 35*).

Fertilisers

Mother Nature is a great gardener. Soil left with nature in control is largely self-sustaining. If a patch of earth is left bare, it will be colonised by wild plants very quickly and depending on conditions, and whether it is grazed or not, a range of species will come to dominate. Where it is grazed animals will return the nutrients they take up in their manure; plants will live and die, also returning what they have taken from the soil.

However, on our intensively cropped plots it is all take, take, take, and we need to constantly top up the available nutrients to feed our plants. Fortunately there are several simple ways to do this.

We have already mentioned that the organic matter we add to improve the soil texture also contains some nutrients, but this is unlikely to be enough to keep your plants happy – unless you garden on the very best loam – and it will be necessary to add more.

During the Second World War the country was blockaded and people had to grow as much of their own produce as possible. In order to get the most from every scrap of land fertilisers were developed. Many of these, such as Growmore (known as National Growmore at the time), are still in use today.

Concerns about adding too much nitrogen-rich man-made fertiliser, which can leach into the water supply, have led to a backlash and many gardeners now use only fertilisers of organic origin.

Man-made feeds – the constituents of which are mainly based on natural minerals – if used carefully and in combination with organic matter, should do no harm and generally give quicker results. It is also worth remembering that too much fertiliser, whether organic or not, can cause pollution.

The choice of fertiliser comes down to personal preference. What is certain is that rising food prices and global shortages will ensure the continued use of man-made fertilisers for the foreseeable future.

Choosing a product

Having decided to use an organic or non-organic feed, or perhaps a combination of both, you will be presented with a bewildering array of products in your local garden centre and on the Internet, many designed for different plants at varying stages of growth, so which do you choose?

Fertilisers generally contain levels of the three main plant nutrients: nitrogen, represented on the packet by the letter N; phosphates (P); and potash (K, from *Kalium*, the Latin for potassium).

Most products also contain minor nutrients (those used by plants in smaller quantities, such as iron) and trace elements (used in tiny quantities, but just as essential for plant growth, such as boron).

All this information must, by law, appear on the packet of any processed fertiliser, whether organic or non-organic, and gives you a clue as to what they are best used for.

Plant nutrients – what do they do?

The following is a simplified guide as to the uses plants have for various nutrients. There are many more minor nutrients and trace elements essential to plant growth, but in most cases these are present in the soil in large enough quantities for us not to have to worry about them.

Nitrogen (N) is mostly concerned with the green parts of the plant and is used to make green chlorophyll, which is important to the plant for the manufacture of food from sunlight.

Deficiencies show as small, pale green leaves, starting with the oldest leaves first; weak plants and poor growth. Nitrogen is easily washed from most soils and quickly used by hungry crops.

Phosphates (P) are important mainly for the internal chemistry of the plant such as in transferring energy from one part of the plant to another. They are often associated with healthy root growth.

Deficiencies are similar to those of nitrogen, but the leaves usually become a dull greeny-blue colour and fall prematurely, starting with the oldest. They are often deficient in wet areas, acid soils and some clays.

Potassium (K) This element is important for developing flowers and fruit.

Deficiencies show as scorching or browning of the leaf tips and edges, and are common on sandy soils where the potassium is easily washed away.

Magnesium (Mg) Like nitrogen, this nutrient is concerned with chlorophyll production in the leaves.

Deficiencies are often seen in fast-growing plants, such as tomatoes, and appear as a yellowing of the leaf between the leaf veins.

Calcium (Ca) is often considered by gardeners as important for adjusting the pH of the soil, but it is a vital plant nutrient in its own right. It is used to build cell walls throughout the plant and is essential for the formation of fruit. It is found in the shoot and root tips where cells are actively dividing.

Deficiencies show as a curling and browning of the shoot tips. Blossom-end rot in tomatoes (where a patch at the flower end of the fruit turns brown and extends, making the fruit inedible) is caused by a lack of calcium. However, it is rare for there to be a shortage of calcium in the soil or potting compost – a lack of water or an interaction with another mineral in the soil is usually the cause (*see Soil improving and pH, page 50*).

DOS AND DON'TS

FERTILISERS

■ Never over-apply plant foods. At best it is a waste, at worst you may scorch the roots and leaves of your plants.

■ Applying regular liquid feeds, for example to tomatoes, can be simplified by feeding at half strength every time you water.

■ Apply top dressings, such as chicken manure pellets, to veg such as beans and onions just before or even during rain as this helps to break them up and wash them in to the soil.

■ Store powdered fertilisers in a cool, dry place in a sealed container. They absorb water from the surrounding air very easily and will lose their effectiveness.

Iron is classed as one of the minor nutrients, meaning that plants use them in smaller quantities, but they are just as necessary for healthy plant growth.

Iron is important for the manufacture of chlorophyll and also has other significant roles.

Deficiency symptoms are similar to those of nitrogen. They are often caused by an excess of calcium and are prominent in lime-hating plants.

Given the information above you can see why it is essential for plants to have a balanced diet if they are to do well. Thankfully, most soils, with the exception of sandy ones, are good at holding on to naturally occurring and applied plant foods – clay is particularly good at this.

It is not too critical which fertiliser you use as long as it contains a range of nutrients. Be aware that some fertiliser products are formulated for different stages of growth. In the early stages you might choose a high nitrogen fertiliser to support healthy shoots and leaves, followed at a later stage by a high potash feed to encourage fruit production and ripening.

The other approach is to use a balanced feed, of which Growmore is the best-known example with an N:P:K content of 7:7:7 to keep matters simple.

Digging

Digging is not just to do with getting rid of weeds before we start to sow new crops. We dig for all kinds of reasons, including breaking up the soil, incorporating manure and organic matter and making the soil into a decent place for our vegetables to grow.

There are a number of no-dig methodologies, which have varying amounts of success, but for the majority of us, digging is the order of the day.

Why dig?

Non-remedial digging is the type of digging necessary to maintain the texture of soil which is already in a satisfactory condition: to keep it aerated, to add organic material and to produce a fine tilth ready for seeding.

Remedial digging is considerably harder work. It is done to get the soil up to scratch in the first place and involves the removal of every bit of perennial weed, as well as changing the soil to make it more productive.

How to dig

- **Small steps** If you are new to digging take your time and dig for only 10 to 15 minutes. By this time you are going to be tired and sore – the muscles around your hips will be tight and your back will be feeling it.
- **Sharp tools** Make sure you feel comfortable using your spade, which is a cutting instrument not a soil-carrying tool. Keep the blade sharp and clean, remove any dirt left on it and give it a coat of oil to keep it spotless.
- **Straight back** The encouragement 'put your back into it' is deadly. Keep your back out of it. Stand straight and use your foot to push the blade into the soil. Then, with straight arms, bent legs and a straight back, straighten your knees and twist the wrists. In this way the soil will lift out and fall to the side. That is all you do. Never bend the back and never use the muscles in the back to lift the spade. The work is done by the legs and less so by the arms.

When you dig, make sure your back is as straight as it can be.

WHEN TO ROTAVATE

Nothing aerates the soil better than a Rotavator. You can create the perfect seedbed – a warm-looking fine tilth – with a Rotavator, but it will not dig to any great depth. Don't get rid of your spades if you have a Rotavator as it will only do a part of the job.

When to dig

The idea of digging is to break the soil, and this is helped by the winter weather. Freezing temperatures, rain and the action of the elements make the soil more friable. The exposure of the buried soil to the cold reduces the action of many pests, and simply turning over of the soil exposes many a chafer grub to the welcome beaks of garden birds. So in many ways, digging is best done after the harvest and before winter. A good habit to get into is to dig over the plot as the crops are removed, and then to manure the land that will have potatoes next year and lime the land that will have brassicas.

Manuring at the earliest stage will give the worms a chance to do their work by dragging the material into the soil, digesting some of the contents and leaving behind fine, nutrient-rich worm casts.

TOP TIP

SOIL ESSENTIALS

We dig in order to give the soil:

Good aeration by turning the soil over.

Good water supply through the addition of rotted manure and compost.

Nutrients from well-rotted compost, chemical fertilisers and rock dust.

Warmth from working the soil into a fine crumbly texture (tilth).

Wildlife to keep the soil healthy.

Hoeing

Dutch hoe

A Dutch hoe, the one we all recognise as a hoe, is a cutting tool with two functions: weeding and making a tilth. A hoe is not a chopping tool and should not be used to cut up clods of soil.

- **Weeding** Use a hoe to chop up weeds along rows of plants. A Dutch hoe has two blades, one either side of the flat blade. Drag the hoe backwards and forwards through the weeds to cut them off at root level.
- **Making a tilth** The same hoe is used to chop up dug soil to make a fine crumbly bed for seeds to grow in. This is achieved in the same way as weeding, but a little deeper.

A Dutch hoe has two blades, cutting on the forwards and the backwards strokes.

Draw hoe

Draw hoes are for drawing soil against a plant, usually potatoes, but sometimes leeks and celery. This is done to shade the plants from light so they do not either green up (as in potatoes) or are blanched (as in leeks).

A draw hoe.

55

Sowing seed

Sowing in modules has made it possible to grow better plants because you handle them less.

Seeds burst into life with the application of water, which activates an enzyme turning starch into sugar, which in turn triggers cell division at the various growing points. The water gets into the seed via a small hole, the micro pile, which happens to be the entry of the pollen tubule when the plant was first pollinated.

You can see this hole on larger seeds, like pumpkin, and as a general rule, if you can see the micro pile, you should place the seed that way down. Although, when sowing pumpkin seeds outside I always sow them on their sides.

Germination

Refer to the packet and germinate at the correct temperature. As a general rule I use tap water to water seeds and seedlings for a number of reasons. One year I washed my greenhouse with an anti-algal cleaner that ran off into the water butts. Some weeks later I came to sow, and not a single seed germinated. It took a long time to work out what had happened.

Allow the tap water to stand for a day or so to remove the fluoride and warm it up.

Temperature

The major reason why plants fail to germinate is a lack of heat. Seeds need the correct temperature to germinate – usually around 14°C. Remember, it can be quite warm in the greenhouse, but if you have repeatedly showered the seeds in cold water, they may germinate more slowly.

Some plants need extra heat for germination, which can be supplied by an external heater, or under-tray heating. These are particularly useful for peppers, some of which need over 20°C to germinate.

Water

Water for seeds must be reasonably clean. Lots of warm water creates a humidity that encourages fungal growth and a problem known as 'damping off', which produces a mushy smelly mess and kills the seedlings. This can be countered by plenty of ventilation to reduce the humidity around your seedlings.

Growing medium

Most people use general-purpose compost for sowing seeds. I prefer to mix leaf mould I have made myself with compost purchased from the allotment shop.

Containers for sowing

Sow in pots or modules, a couple of seeds to each pot or cell, and remove the weakest seedling. Then grow the plant on until it is ready to be transplanted to its final position.

Always put seeds to the hand, and sow from there. Never pour seeds directly from the packet to the compost – you might lose them all!

Young seedlings getting air to reduce the chance of 'damping off'.

Modules for sowing.

How to transplant

When your plant has grown too big for the pot or module it is time to pot on to a larger pot, or to put it outside in its growing spot.

■ **Transplanting to a pot** Fill the new pot with compost and use a pencil to make a hole ready to take the roots of the seedling. Holding only the leaf, use the pencil to lever the seedling out of its pot. Then use the pencil to guide the root into the hole you made earlier. Gently but firmly secure the plant into its new position. Water well.

■ **Transplanting to a growing position** It may be necessary to harden your plants off, acclimatising them to the generally colder (but hopefully warming) conditions outside: take the modules outside in the morning and bring them in at night. A week of this will not only have the plants ready for the outside world, but if done at the end of May there should be no more frosts. Then dig a hole to receive the new plant. Loosen the compost in the module, and push up with your finger from below to push the plant out. Holding the leaves, pop the plant into its new home. Firm in and water well.

Propagation

There are a number of propagation techniques useful on the allotment from simple division of plants like rhubarb to grafting of apples and pears. The thing about propagation is the end result – the final crop or bloom – is genetically identical to the parent stock. Therefore, a fantastically succulent strawberry, for example, will be just as succulent, assuming the propagated plants will be grown in similar conditions.

Propagating by runners

A runner is like a rhizome, only it 'runs' along the surface of the soil. You can see them on strawberries as stems, flat and over 30cm (12in) long.

About half way along a mature runner (60cm/24in long) you will find a little shoot. Fill an 8cm (3in) pot with compost and place the shoot (still attached to the runner) on the compost. Anchor it down with a pebble on the compost. Within a month the shoot will have set roots and will have begun the process of growing a new shoot. When it looks big enough to survive, cut away the runner and you will have a new strawberry plant. It will also be free of the disease problems affecting the parent plant.

This is a form of layering, which works with larger shrubs. Take a plant like buddleia, for example. If you push a branch to the ground and place a large pebble to hold it in place, roots will form where the stem touches the ground.

Hardwood cuttings

These are an easy way to increase your stock of plants such as gooseberries and currants. I have always found they root better in a bucket than pushed into the soil.

Simply take off a branch of this year's growth. Cut off the growing tip and remove any leaves. Trim just below a bud so you have about 30cm (12in) of twig.

In a bucket, mix 25% sand and 75% good quality compost. Push the cuttings into the compost and keep in a cool greenhouse or a sheltered spot. Expect anything from 50% to root next spring. I rarely use rooting powder with these.

Shoot cuttings

New growth, a twig or a leaf, is rather exciting because it has sufficient recovery power to set roots or shoots easily when removed. Shoot cuttings are simple to take. Cut off the growing tip of a shoot a good 15cm (6in) down the stem. Remove all but the top couple of leaves and dip the end in hormone rooting powder (it contains fungicide which stops the end of the plant rotting). Pop the cutting into some moist but not damp compost and sand mixture (75% compost) in an 8cm (3in) pot and place a polythene bag over the plant, fixing it with a rubber band on the pot.

Heel cuttings

These are like shoot cuttings, but instead you pull (or cut) away a shoot as it comes from a branch and place the cut stem (heel) into the compost, having dipped it in rooting powder.

Leaf cuttings

Few plants on the allotment are propagated in this way. I have made coleus, begonia and streptocarpus Christmas presents using this method.

Cut a leaf into two or more pieces and push them into compost in a tray. Do this in June and fill a seed tray with the cuttings. Water and keep fairly moist and place a plastic bag around the tray to keep up the humidity. At a temperature of 20°C you will find the cuttings rooting in about six weeks and they will be ready to pot on by the end of the summer.

Taking a hardwood cutting.

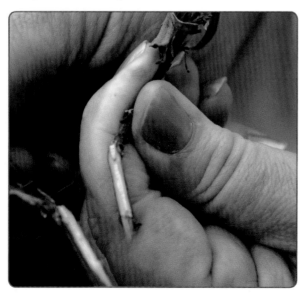

A rhubarb crown ready to divide into two with a sharp knife.

Dividing

After about five to eight years a rhubarb plant will need to be split, its leaves will have become crowded. Dig it up and find the rhizome off which there will be a number of bud-bearing protuberances. Simply cut between two to create two plants. You can frequently divide the rhizomes into three or four plants – the individual pieces are known as crowns. Replant the crowns in nutrient rich soil, or give one away to a friend.

Grafting

If you cut a tree branch, or any plant for that matter, you will see lots of rings. Once a branch is one year old (on woody plants) you will see a distinct line just inside the bark layer and between the water and food carrying vessels. This layer is called cambium. It is where cells divide and create new wood, water tubes, bark and so on.

If the cambium of the graft and the stock (that is the plant you are grafting onto) are touching, the graft will grow into the stock and grow as though it has always been a part of it. The hormones in the cambium will change because of the presence of the graft, and consequently the join will be strong. It takes a while for this to work and so the two pieces need to be taped together.

The graft is traditionally known as a scion and the plant you are grafting on is called the stock.

CLEFT GRAFT

This is used to graft whole plants onto rootstocks (*see box*). Choose an unblemished part of the stem and make a clean, horizontal cut through the rootstock, about 25cm (10in) above the root. Then make a vertical cut into that, about 3cm (1in) deep. Choose a scion that is just coming out of dormancy. Make a sharp wedge at the end of it and push it firmly into the 'cleft' you made in the rootstock and tape it up.

A cleft graft.

WHAT MAKES A ROOTSTOCK WORK?

Rootstocks work because the stock and the scion forced onto it are members of the same botanical family. Apples, roses and pears, for instance, are all members of the same family and this contributes to their success. Rootstocks have been of most use in the apple industry and create trees of varying height and aspect. The main UK rootstocks for apples are M25, MM106, M26, M9 and M27. M25 gives a full-size, old-fashioned tree. (*See Fruit: Rootstocks, page 142.*)

You can see the rootstock where it joins to the stem, or scion.

Tools

How to buy tools

A good tool is a boon, and should last forever, so buy the best you can and look after it. Ideally, the shaft should be wood. Look for the grain – it should run parallel down the shaft with no knots. There should not be any knobbly or sharp bits on the shaft or handle that might pinch, catch, or cause a blister.

The business end of the tool should be strong, made from steel, fitted seamlessly with the shaft and have no wobble or blemish.

Look for a smooth, even grain in the wood with no kinks, and nothing sharp.

How to care for tools

- When you have used a tool, clean it. Don't leave soil on the blade.
- A bucket of sand with motor oil in it will suffice to oil the blade.
- You should sharpen the blade at least twice a year – most tools are cutting objects, and it is a help if they are really sharp.
- Oil the shaft with linseed every now and again and hang the tool rather than standing it on the floor.
- Always take your tools home if you don't want them being stolen.

TOP TIP

A SECURE SHED IS AN OPEN SHED

Leave your shed door open, so people know there is nothing of value in it.

Spade

The spade is the main cutting tool in the garden. They come in various sizes and the spade you choose should fit you, feel balanced in your hands, and should be strong enough to do the job but light enough not to wear you out.

There is no such thing as a 'lady's spade' – just large ones and smaller ones. Therefore you should be perfectly happy with how it feels before you buy it, large or small. Clearly spades are for digging but they are also a cutting tool — so keep it sharp. Once dug don't lift the material too high – you have to learn how to dig with as much efficiency as your own frame allows.

- Don't do too much at one time
- Don't use a spade to carry material
- Don't overload the blade
- Don't use a spade as a shovel - see below

Garden fork

This is a tool for breaking up soil, from aerating lawns to breaking clods. In general it should be used on soil that has recently been dug with a spade. It is not a digging tool – it doesn't cut through the soil. If you try to dig with a garden fork you will constantly be breaking the soil apart using your muscles without the efficiency of a blade.

Use the fork in the second stage of digging - to create great beds.

Dutch hoe

This is a cutting tool for making a fine soil structure for seedlings to be planted in and for breaking annual weeds around crops. It is used by keeping the blade in contact with the soil at all times, rather than chopping, where the forces are translated into shockwaves in your arms.

Some Dutch hoes are wide bladed with two cutting surfaces, one on the push and the other on the pull.

Cultivator

This tool is for breaking up soil in a bed. Particularly useful in raised beds, Use it like a rake and fork combined to break up the soil. If your soil is on the light side, this tool is excellent for breaking it up.

Draw hoe

As the name implies, this is for drawing soil - particularly against potatoes, to cover the tubers, or leeks or celery. It is not to be used for cutting into the soil or chopping, but it is such a useful tool, it is well worth the expense.

Shovel

This is not a cutting tool, though it is often used as one. It is for carrying and moving materials, loading into a wheelbarrow and so on. It has a measured pan and is shaped for easy pouring. Used as a spade, it cuts well, but is not as efficient as a sharp, flat bladed spade. Long handle shovels are frequently used for digging – you get a better leverage and if you are unhappy using a conventional spade – seek one of these out.

Garden Rake

This tool has one real job, and several others. Its design job is for finishing beds for sowing, smoothing the surface, breaking fine clods and removing stones. A good rake will last a lifetime so long as you avoid the tendency of using it instead of a hoe. Tempting as it is to break up the soil with a rake, this will simply weaken the join, and you will end up with a broken tool.

Other tools

Secateurs
Used for pruning and deadheading, an expensive pair will last forever. Keep them well oiled. In use I always give them a wipe between plants to avoid passing disease from one to another.

Garden line
This is possibly the best tool in the garden - you use it to create straight lines!

Trowels and hand forks
These are for creating small holes for planting. Buy one which has a rule stamped on the side so you can get an idea of how deep to dig. Remember – these are not heavy duty digging tools, just aids for planting.

Dibber
This is a stick, albeit a wide one. Frequently made from the 'T' of an old spade. It has a point for pushing into the ground, and is ideal for planting. Never push sets or garlic into the soil - use a dibber.

Pen knife
A really good knife has myriad uses on the plot – keep it sharp, and if you have anything stored in the shed – make it a sharpening stone as the average tool thief won't recognize it anyway.

Make a raised bed

Raised beds are great for avoiding back problems and this one is ideal for growing herbs. The same technique can be used to make a larger bed if required.

TOOLS AND MATERIALS

You will need:

Eight 92cm (3ft) lengths of 230mm x 22mm (9in x 1in) timber

Four stakes: 45mm x 45mm (approx 2in square) and 60cm (2ft) long. (See note at step 7)

Sandpaper and sanding block (or a small plane to chamfer edges)

Hammer

Nails: 65mm galvanised ovals

Drill and 3mm drill bit

Tape measure

Pencil

Heavy lump hammer for bracing and knocking in posts

Note: you will need a saw to cut timber, and to put points on the stakes, if your timber supplier hasn't done this for you.

1 Sand or plane all rough edges to ensure there are no splinters.

3 Drill holes at the marked points. This allows nails to pass through the timber without splitting it. Keep the drill upright so nails run straight.

2 Measure and mark where to drill holes for the nails. This is probably the trickiest bit. Although the bed is effectively square, it's best to look at two of the sides as being the front and the back and the other two opposites as being the sides of the bed.

The front and back boards will overlap the stakes by 22mm (the thickness of a board). The boards at the two sides can butt directly against this overlap, or you can leave a 5mm gap so water doesn't collect along the end grain of the boards.

Use the tape measure and pencil to mark two nailing points at each end of the front and back boards. These points should be 47mm in from the ends of the board and 30mm in from the long edges of the board.

Mark points 20mm in from the ends and 20mm in from the long edges of the remaining boards.

These different measurements ensure that nails don't collide and that they are placed centrally on the stakes.

4 Assemble the front section: nail two boards (with holes at 47mm x 30mm) onto two stakes keeping the whole thing as square as possible. Repeat for the back section.

5 The front and back sections can be knocked into the ground and the boards added on to the two sides afterwards. This involves careful measuring to make sure the side boards fit perfectly (allowing the 5mm gap). Alternatively, the bed can be assembled before the stakes are knocked into the ground. If you choose the latter method, you will need to enrol another pair of hands to hold everything straight.

In either case, use a heavy lump hammer, or something similar, to brace the back of the stake when hammering.

6 If you intend to paint the structure do so now while all points are accessible. It's possible to leave timber unpainted and this will darken with age and exposure to the weather. The boards are thick enough to last many years even if they are untreated.

7 Knock the stakes into the ground to anchor the bed in place.
Note: If your garden is on an exposed, windy site, then long stakes will hold the bed in position. If your site is sheltered, you may well get away with just sitting the bed on the ground and can use shorter stakes.

8 Fill the bed with compost and plant with your favourite herbs.

63

Make a bean frame

This structure avoids the tangle of stems often found at the top of a typical bean frame. It is easy to dismantle at the end of the season and should last for several years.

MATERIALS & TOOLS

You will need:
14 Bamboo canes at least 210cm (7ft) long
2 pieces timber 50mm x 20mm x 155cm (2in x 1in x 5ft)
2 pieces of timber 50mm x 50mm x 80cm
   (2in x 2in x 32in)
2 pieces of timber 50mm x 50mm x 220cm
   (2in x 2in x 7ft 3in)
Drill plus 5mm drill bit
Screwdriver (or screwdriver bit for drill)
Screws: 2 @ 5 x 100mm (4in)
          4 @ 5 x 60mm (2½in)
Flexible garden wire, or strong rot-proof string
Sandpaper

1 Sand all rough edges on the timber.

2 Assemble the top of the frame. The top of the frame is basically a rectangle, formed by screwing the two 155cm (5ft) lengths and the two 80cm (32in) lengths of timber together. Drill a guide hole 25mm (1in) in from each end of the 155cm lengths. Use the 60mm (2½in) screws to fix through the guide holes and to screw into the ends of the 80cm (32in) lengths. There should be no difficulty screwing into the end grain.

3 Fix the upright posts. Posts are positioned at the mid points of the 80cm (32in) pieces. Again, drill a guide hole through the 80cm (32in) piece of wood and use the 100mm (4in) screws to go through this and into the end of the 220cm (7ft 3in) length. Don't drill into the upright post — it will be easy enough to get a firm grip in the end grain.

4 Put up the frame. Dig holes to accommodate the two upright posts. The holes should be deep enough to bury at least 30cm (1ft) depth of the posts. You may need two people to locate the posts and raise the structure into an upright position. One person should hold the frame steady while the other packs small stones and earth into the holes around the posts. Stamp down with your boot to pack the holes as firmly as possible. The frame should be steady at this point, but the bamboos will provide extra stability.

5 Tie in the bamboo poles. Space the bamboo poles at equal distances along the two sides of the frame. The poles can be pushed into the ground until the top comes to a level position above the frame. Use wire to tie the top of the canes against the wooden frame.

6 Plant beans at an even spacing around the canes.

How to string onions

1 Make sure onion stems and skins are completely dry before stringing.

2 Cut a 140cm length of string. If you are in any doubt about the strength of your string, then use double thickness – a full rope of onions is pretty heavy.

Knock a nail in just above head height. If you don't have a suitable beam then rest a plank of wood against the wall and knock a nail into this – the string won't hang as freely, but it will still work fine. Knot the ends of your string and hang it over the nail with the knotted end at the top.

3 Make a loop for the first onion by turning the bottom of the string upwards to form two loops through which a finger can be slotted.

6 Keep adding more onions by twisting the stems around both strings. Work your way round the central strings so that onions are evenly balanced on all sides. You are aiming for closely packed onions and the string should be virtually hidden.

7 Keep adding more onions until you are about 15cm away from the knot at the top.

8 Cut off any dangling leaves and roots to give a clear string of onions.

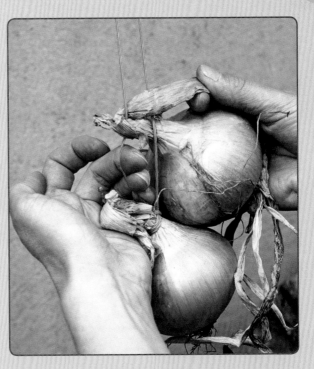

4 Choose a large onion and thread the neck through these two loops. This onion will hang at the base of your string and other onions will be threaded above it.

5 Take a second onion and twist the neck around both strands of string. Try to keep the onion bulb close in to the string – if you allow too much slack you will get a floppy looking bunch of onions rather than a tight rope. Always remember to twist the neck round both strings, or your onions won't be held firmly in place and they may fall out.

9 Hang onions in a dry, cool place if possible. A shed or unheated bedroom is ideal, but one or two strings look attractive in the kitchen.

GREENHOUSES AND POLYTUNNELS

You can do a lot with a polytunnel or greenhouse. They make
gardening much easier at the extremes of the season.

In the 1970s, during a busy period of slum clearance in UK cities, there was a significant increase in the numbers of greenhouses on allotments. The art of running an allotment is the core of self-sufficiency and inventive making-do and these greenhouses were the epitome of just that. Window frames, old bricks, doors and paving were 'pilfered' (perhaps we should say 'rescued') from demolition sites to build make-do greenhouses. Some of them are still standing today.

Despite difficult periods, many allotments have shiny new greenhouses and polytunnels, and the small clumps of horticultural fleece splash the plots with misty light. There is a mania for growing under cover these days.

Positioning

All in a row

Some sites insist that greenhouses and polytunnels are lined up at the same point of each plot. There are good reasons for this:

Out of reach Tunnels at the periphery of the site are vulnerable to attack from off-site. I once had a greenhouse destroyed by schoolchildren playing football at lunchtime. It was not their fault, they needed to learn how to kick a ball, it was my fault. A policy that kept my greenhouse out of reach would have been good.

Light, space and wind Greenhouses and polytunnels affect the amount of light and space for each plot. A huge polytunnel casts a shadow, and also blocks out wind. I saw a plot that had never had white spot on onions until the neighbour erected a tunnel. The effect of the wind had kept the plot dry enough to prevent white rot, but the tunnel acted as a windbreak and the soil became damp enough to encourage the growth and the onions were spoilt.

Designated areas

Some allotments allow greenhouses only in a designated area, leaving the rest of the plots flat and often fence-free. Others have polytunnels in certain places, or a community polytunnel in which everyone gets a space, while others allow them anywhere. On one site I saw polytunnels and greenhouses placed around the outer rim of the site. They had problems with vandalism because the outer wall, which belonged to a defunct gas company, collapsed leaving the structures exposed.

On your plot

If you can position your greenhouse anywhere on your allotment, undertake a survey of your site. A greenhouse needs light and space, so placing it out of the way, under trees or against a wall, is not the answer. You could do well by placing it in a damp area, using raised beds inside the greenhouse to compensate. Nothing beats the convenience of having your own greenhouse on your own plot, and not having to walk to the other side of the site to garden in it.

Some sites make you place all your tunnels and greenhouses in a row, usually to keep shadows at bay.

A well organised winter greenhouse – notice the crate and shale floor.

Running a greenhouse

There is no doubt that the greenhouse is a boon, and a polytunnel is an even bigger boon to the vegetable and fruit gardener. The greenhouse provides a light, warm place for growing plants that are temperature-sensitive or simply do not do well in a buffeted, wet, frequently cold environment.

Why do I need a greenhouse?

■ To grow crops such as tomatoes, peppers, cucumbers, melons and grapes.
■ To overwinter delicate plants, such as potted camellias, and to have a place for cuttings and seedlings to grow.
■ The greenhouse or polytunnel extends the growing period – something to be enjoyed more in a tunnel because of its larger floor area. You can start thinking about growing crops out of season, and by carefully compartmentalising the area you can sow in one part, grow on in another.
■ You can achieve almost perfect produce – it is not messed about by wind and rain, there is less likelihood of attracting certain pests, and when pests do arrive they can be dealt with more easily by using organic methods.

First principles

■ Keep it clean, well organised and uncluttered. This is the most important point in keeping a polytunnel or greenhouse. Avoid the temptation to use the area as a place to plant combined with an extension to the shed. Piles of wood, seed trays, tools, pots, packets of seeds, fertiliser, canes and all the myriad things we use on the plot should go in the shed. They introduce hazards from falling, they encourage disease and they attract and harbour rats.

Chrysanthemums in November fill your allotment with colour.

A packed greenhouse with the doors open – notice the side
windows open too.

- Clear out the greenhouse or tunnel at least twice a year –
so far as plants allow – and disinfect the glassware,
shelving and staging. If you are able, use a horticultural
disinfectant on the path and soil and leave it a couple of
weeks to degenerate before planting.
- Any compost you bring into the tunnel or greenhouse
should be well rotted. Do not bring in compost that
smells of must or the riverbed as it will contain fungi.
Sterilising compost is easy on a tin lid over a fire.
- Do not store seeds of any kind in the greenhouse – it gets
too hot for them, and you will have reduced germination.
- Where possible, store anything you do keep in the
greenhouse or tunnel off the ground – you need to
maximise your growing space.

Ventilation
IN THE GREENHOUSE

Greenhouses work by trapping heat that otherwise would
have risen into the higher atmosphere. This trapping of heat
causes two major problems: the structure gets hot and the
heat draws moisture from the soil, so it becomes humid too.

Heat and humidity are the two most important factors in
the growth of fungal infections. You need to replace the air
in the structure without losing too much heat, while keeping
the temperature within parameters suitable for good
growth, normally around 20–22°C.

A thermostatically controlled arm that opens the top
window in a greenhouse is an excellent aid. When it is hot
the window is fully open, and when it goes cold at night it
closes. Combined with the door being open a little, hot air
can escape and keep the space in reasonable condition.

It sometimes becomes necessary to open the door fully if
the temperature is high. If you are able fit a fly screen – one
of those screens made from lots of plastic strands – air
will circulate but many airborne pests will be deterred
from entering.

IN THE POLYTUNNEL

There are a number of ingenious ways to ventilate a tunnel.
First, and simplest, is to have two doors, open both and get
a bit of a breeze going through the tunnel (this is imperative
if you are growing sweetcorn indoors as it is the only way
you will get germination).

You can also build side screens into your tunnel. This is an
arrangement in which the polythene is attached to a base
rail that is not at the bottom of the tunnel, but about a
metre (yard) off the ground. From the rail to the floor a green
mesh is placed, behind which there is a roll of polythene that
rises and falls using a crank. This system allows as much or as
little ventilation as you need. On a hot day the plants are
kept at ambient temperatures while at the same time they

A homemade tunnel with side ventilation.

remain in a perfect growing environment. On a cold day, with the plastic down, the polytunnel is a good 7–10°C warmer than outside.

Watering systems

Ever since greenhouses have become popular the general instruction has been to dampen down the path by splashing water all over the place. The water will evaporate, cooling the greenhouse and increasing the humidity. The problem with this is that the increased humidity (and warmth) can promote fungal growth. We now know that blight lives on the surface of the soil in spore form and once splashed with water and higher humidity, it can burst into life. Spreading water about the greenhouse or polytunnel can lead to blight, especially if you have brought it in via the potato patch. How many of you have had blight on your tomatoes?

Overhead watering systems are popular and convenient, especially when you are away on holiday and you can ask someone to water for you just by turning on the tap for a

Keep the door open when necessary.

www.northernpolytunnels.co.uk

few minutes. Personally, I prefer those with drip tubes that feed individual plants without covering the whole place with water. There are a number of these, from simple bags that you hang from a crop bar to computerised, programmable systems that cost a fortune.

If you have an overhead watering system you will find it is best used in conjunction with good ventilation.

Heating

On the allotment it is highly unlikely you will have a source of electricity and so the only power available to you will be sunlight or paraffin, unless you have a wood burner and you are not in a smokeless area. I have seen many allotments with sheds and greenhouses with wood burners, even some with heating systems feeding hot water into beds.

If you are going to run a heated greenhouse or polytunnel, think about keeping a part of it unheated, or having another, cold greenhouse to cater for plants that need frost-free but cool conditions. An unheated greenhouse will be 10°C hotter than ambient temperature in the summer, around 5°C in the winter. Plants such as grapes do not need to overwinter in the warm as they are used to very harsh frosts around the world.

Aim to keep the temperature at around 5°C on the coldest nights. A single paraffin heater will heat a small greenhouse, 180 x 120cm (6 x 4ft). A larger polytunnel will need three heaters. I prefer to use two or more small heaters because they have a low profile and a bigger distribution of heat than one large one.

NATURAL HEATING METHODS

There are a number of things you can do to increase the efficiency of your greenhouse or tunnel in terms of heat.
Heat sink If you make a good, heavy path, one that comes above the level of the soil, it becomes a heat sink, warming during the day and releasing this heat at night. You can place plants in pots on a piece of insulating material on the path and they will remain above freezing on cold nights.
Water butt Similarly, an internal water butt will do exactly the same thing if you place plants around the base of the butt. Always keep a lid on the butt (please note our comments on water safety, see Water, page 45).
Insulation placed around the coldest parts of the greenhouse – particularly the door where draughts get in – makes a real difference.
Nightlight If you have hollow concrete blocks, a nightlight in the block keeps that area warm, and you can keep plants in pots around it free from frost. The block acts as a radiator and if the light burns itself out, the block will remain warm for some time.

Buying greenhouses and polytunnels

The various designs of greenhouses on the market are easy to spot and essentially you get what you pay for, especially in terms of size.

When it comes to polytunnels there is a lot to consider. Of course, you get a lot more coverage for your money, but there are drawbacks. If the tunnel cannot be sited away from the public, you might need to consider some form of protection. Even if your allotments are at the back of a sleepy village, they are not necessarily safe. I visited a site in a village that would have looked good on a chocolate box, and its polytunnel had been most horribly damaged.

Polytunnels work by having a taut skin. You can bury the skin in the ground to keep it taut, or use the more recent method of attaching the skin to base rails that you stand on to tighten the skin before fixing it to the hoops. This system is usually more expensive, but well worth the effort.

Another kind of base rail, one that goes half way up the hoops, allows for a mesh side for ventilation, which can be covered by a curtain of polythene which can be raised or lowered to provide varying amounts of ventilation *(see Ventilation, page 72)*.

One of the benefits of polytunnels is crop bars, which can be super for growing tomatoes against, or making hanging baskets.

This homemade covered bed is a halfwayhouse between a greenhouse and a cold frame.

Cold frames are very effective alternatives to a greenhouse – especially if you are working on half a plot.

UNDER COVER PLANTS

A guide to some of the plants you can grow in the greenhouse or tunnel.

Seeds and seedlings

In the UK we have long grown tomatoes in greenhouses. I cannot think why as tomatoes often do just as well outside, but they do need warmth for starting off. This is possibly the most important use of the greenhouse – providing a warm environment for seed sowing and the growing of seedlings.

Staging is an important part of the process, and many people use a plastic-covered shelving system to stack trays of seedlings. This means you can have a cool greenhouse for other purposes and a warmed, plastic-covered inner shelf that can be kept at the appropriate temperature, normally around 14°C.

Make sure you are able to provide ventilation once the seeds have germinated, especially on warm days, or the problem of damping-off will appear.

Grapes

In a greenhouse there is usually not that much room except for a few tomatoes, a number of salads and maybe some peppers. The polytunnel is a different affair. It is important to plan what is going into your tunnel, and for me this starts with grapes. The system of growing grapes down the centre of the top of the tunnel provides shade for the rest of the plants in the summer.

Many people first buy a polytunnel or greenhouse with the idea of growing grapes.

Grapes grow best in areas where the spring is dry, the summer is hot and the winter is cold. In our recent past, spring is damp, summer is wet and the winter is mild, but with a little shelter there is no reason why this vigorous climbing plant cannot be grown with great success.

Keys to success
- Fruit is produced on one-year-old growth
- The plant will bleed if you cut it in the growing period
- The fruit will rot if the atmosphere is too moist
- Plants like a good feed once a year
- Vines prefer to be cold in the winter

Remember that whatever pruning regime you use, you need to have some shoots that, this year, will grow leaves but no fruit, so that next year they can produce fruit. All pruning takes place at the end of the season when the plant is not actively growing. If your tunnel or greenhouse is heated you are best to grow grapes as standards in large tubs so they can be placed outside in the cold.

Training systems

There are a number of culture systems based on making either a single stem (cordon) or a double one. The vines are either trained on a vertical wire system, so that the wires are at heights of 30cm (12in) to support the cordons, or a single wire in the top of the tunnel.

Single cordon vines

- Plant your vine outside the tunnel and train the vine through the plastic (or a hole in the greenhouse glass) to the inside. Allow it to grow unhindered.
- The soil should be well dug and mixed with plenty of well-rotted manure and compost. Traditionally, vines were planted above a rotting dead sheep.
- Stake the vine outside the tunnel or greenhouse and attach a wire to a frame indoors, along which you will train the plant.
- In the summer of the first year allow the plant to grow, and pinch back any lateral shoots to around five leaves.

Grapes in the greenhouse, ready to be trained along the ridge roof.

Grapes grown as a cordon along wires against the glass.

- When the leaves have fallen off in the winter, cut back the main shoot by just a little more than half and cut the laterals to a single bud each.
- In the summer of the second year treat the plant like you did the previous summer; tie in the main shoot and build your frame of wires. Take out any flowers that form.
- The following winter cut the main shoot back to old wood and the laterals to a strong bud each. So, in effect you have strengthened and prepared your plant ready for producing laterals that you will now tie in the following spring and summer.
- The buds will then grow out, and the resultant growth is trained along the wires.
- In the third summer allow one bunch of grapes per lateral shoot to form, and any sub-laterals that form keep to a single leaf. In the winter, when the grapes are taken and the leaves have fallen, cut the laterals to two buds. It is these buds you will use next year and so on.

Care
Indoor vines do well if they are fed with tomato fertiliser each month from a couple of weeks after they have burst into life in the spring until the grapes are ready for picking. Since the bark is fibrous, all kinds of pests overwinter, so scrape the bark away inside the tunnel or greenhouse.

If you are growing grapes in Scotland then it is a good idea to heat the greenhouse to 4°C from mid-winter onwards. This will give them a good head start.

Harvest
The problem with grapes is that they are full of sugar and unless you have good ventilation between the berries, *Penicillium* will infect the bunches. You can use scissors (some growers have special scissors just for the purpose) to thin out the berries so that the others can grow unencumbered and a good air flow around the grapes is achieved.

The cardinal rule on harvesting is to cut off the piece of lateral they are growing from so that you do not have to touch the grapes and either contaminate or damage them.

Diseases
We have already spoken of fungal infection. It comes in three forms:

Botrytis occurs in wet conditions and is kept at bay by good pruning.

Downy mildew occurs where the temperature is really hot and the greenhouse or tunnel is very humid.

Powdery mildew forms on the leaves and fruit. You can prune it away, keep the tunnel or greenhouse really clean and spray with Bordeaux Mixture, developed by French monks just for this purpose 300 years ago and it is still considered to be an organic cure by many.

Cucumbers

- If you can maintain a minimum soil temperature of 13–15°C then you can start to sow cucumbers as early in the year as you like. I plant them in 12cm (5in) pots, making two holes in each with a dibber. Push a seeds into the side of each hole, sprinkle compost over them and water lightly. Pop them in a propagator and they should germinate within ten days.

- A couple of weeks later, discard the weakest-growing plant – unless there is no real difference between them, in which case I pot one on into another pot.

- Keep the plants watered, but not wet, for another month and they will be ready to be planted in their growing positions – which for me means ring culture pots. They might well outgrow the propagator, so just move them to a table – keep them off the floor as it is cooler down there.

- When the plants are about six weeks old they go into ring culture pots, usually pushed into a growbag. I have also used the straw bale method, which involved cutting a hole, about the size of a 250mm (10in) pot, in a straw bale, filling it with compost, and then planting the cucumber in it.

- Cucumbers need support and I usually use a net mounted against a support. In the polytunnel I have used strings tied to the crop bar to secure them, but I still prefer a net because it is easier to support the fruits, and much better than messing about with pieces of string.

Temperature

Try to make the air temperature at night as close to 16–18°C as you can. I have divided my tunnel into two parts, so I only have to heat a small area. I was lucky, I managed to get hold of one of those heavy plastic doors that you can just walk through – it works a treat.

Care

Treat cucumbers like tomatoes (except they do not grow trusses). Make sure they are well watered and fed at least once a week. You can buy drip-feed bags and you can add fertiliser (high in potash – like tomato feed). I used this with fertiliser from the garden centre, diluted to a quarter of the strength. I set it to drip once every 30 seconds while I was away for a week and it seemed to work a treat, and there was still plenty of feed/water left when I got back.

Varieties

I have grown 'Telegraph' and 'Conqueror' of the old types, and I love their strong flavour. I remove the male flowers that appear, leaving the female ones to grow. The newer F1 varieties that I have grown, 'Carmen F1' and 'Euphya F1', only have female flowers.

These days you don't need knobbly cucumbers.

Tomatoes

We grow tomatoes indoors more than anything else in greenhouses and polytunnels around the country. It is a staple crop we seem always to have time for over other, possibly more valuable crops. Personally, I am of the opinion that you should grow what you like on the plot, not simply those things that are expensive in the shops, consequently the greenhouse will be full of tomatoes for a long time to come.

- So long as you can keep the temperature in the right zone, 12–14°C, you can sow seeds any time. However, it is possibly best to wait until early April.
- Sow in modules of seed compost, two seeds to a cell, discarding the slowest growing one.
- Transplant seedlings into 8cm (3in) pots of compost as soon as the first true leaves have appeared.
- When the plant is a hand's breadth high, pot on to a 10cm (4in) pot and from there, probably around the end of May or early June, plant out into its final growing position.

Growbags

I usually use growbags, growing two plants per bag. This way I do not have to worry about soil-borne pests and if I choose I can grow in the same position year on year.

Ring culture pots are the traditional way to grow tomatoes. These are a pot without a bottom, allowing you to water inside the pot without splashing it all over the plant.

Watering

Your success with tomatoes depends on three things: water, feed and warmth, which we have already discussed. Tomatoes should never be allowed to run dry. Watering should be even over the whole summer: water, using the same amount, every two or three days. This is even more important when the fruits are on the plant. A period of dryness followed by remedial watering causes the fruits to split as they swell with water and makes them susceptible to blossom end rot, where the flower rots on the fruit before it falls off, leaving a black ring of rot and a useless tomato.

Don't forget that outdoor tomatoes often do better than indoor ones – so plant both!

Feeding

There are many who make their own tea for feeding tomatoes – a pillow of comfrey or manure, left in water like a teabag. Personally I don't usually do this for two reasons: first (and probably the most important), I can't abide the smell; second, I do not like to introduce what is basically rotting material into the greenhouse or polytunnel. I believe it could easily introduce fungal infections.

I use a simple (and cheap) tomato fertiliser from the allotments shop. It has all the nutrition the plant needs and all the trace elements too, which many homebrew fertilisers miss out on. Feed once a fortnight until the flowers appear, once a week until the fruits are a decent size.

Pruning

Tomatoes will grow and divide and produce lots of vegetative growth – huge vines that spread everywhere. The amount of fruit they produce can be increased by pruning.

- First, where a leaf comes from a stem, a bud will appear, and turn into a branch. This is called a side shoot. These should always be removed.
- You will need to support your tomatoes, and I find the best way to do this in a polytunnel is to attach a string to crop bars fastened to the hoops. Canes can also be used (after a collision between the top of a cane and my eye, I started to place yoghurt pots on them). Tie the tomatoes where the leaves come out for best support. If you are using string tied to the bottom of the plant, simply wrap the tomato around the string.
- The next pruning you need to do is to stop the plant growing too tall – this is more about the quality of fruit rather than the size of the plant. The flowers form on vines called trusses. Each truss can hold up to a dozen fruits. Stop the plant from producing any more when you have your required number of trusses. If you allow three to develop you will have very tasty tomatoes. If you allow four the crop will still be good and flavoursome. If you allow five trusses the flavour might be slightly reduced and, in my opinion, six trusses are too much. I usually stick to four or five trusses per plant. When you have what you need, cut out the growing tip of the plant and no more trusses will appear – assuming you take out all the side shoots, which can have trusses of their own.

TUMBLER TOMATOES

The variety 'Tumbler' cascades downwards and is the only one that grows this way with any success. It is perfect for growing in hanging baskets. I neither prune nor check these tomatoes – simply water and feed in the usual way.

Varieties

Beef tomatoes are as big as your hand and perfect for slicing for burgers and sandwiches: 'Beef master'.

Cherry tomatoes are small varieties that explode in the mouth and are perfect for salads: 'Bambino', 'Gardener's Delight'.

Salad standard is the ordinary tomato, a good all-rounder: 'Moneymaker', 'Ailsa Craig'.

Plum are best for sauces and cooking: 'Roma', 'San Mazarno'.

TOP TIP

HOW TO RIPEN TOMATOES

In around the second week of August, all your tomatoes will have reached a good size, even if they are green. Remove the leaves – after all, the toms are not going to get any bigger – and reduce the watering to once a week, and reduce the quantity. This will encourage ripening, but will also cut down on the possibility of fungal infections by lowering the humidity.

Remember to pick up any dead leaves or other debris that might introduce disease.

Underripe Romano tomatoes, in October!

Chillies and peppers

I almost always treat chillies and peppers as though they were tomatoes, but there are some differences in the way they are grown.

The Scoville Scale

A chilli is full of oils, which give the 'heat' to the fruit. The reaction between mouth, lips and skin, and chilli oil can cause a very serious irritation.

Mild chillies have a Scoville number less than 1,000. The hottest are over 50,000, the very hottest over 850,000. When you buy seeds, bear the Scoville number in mind (and for goodness sake, wash your hands before going to the toilet).

Sowing

■ Chillies should be sown like tomatoes from the end of February to April. Use good quality general-purpose compost and sow in modules, two seeds per unit, pinching out the weakest plant.

■ Use the best compost you can find. I have had the best results after sterilising this compost in the oven.

■ Keep the compost damp but not wet, and if you are using a propagator, lift the lid for a couple of hours to reduce the humidity. They need warm soil to germinate, over 20°C and some need a few degrees more.

■ Put them in the lightest part of the greenhouse or polytunnel, and aim for them to grow slowly rather than bolting in the dark – give them plenty of sunshine.

Potting-on

Pot on to an 8cm (3in) pot using good quality compost as soon as the second leaves are visible. Allow the plant to grow until it is about 15cm (6in) and pot on to a 30cm (12in) pot. You can use a growbag instead of a pot if you prefer.

Growing

The important thing about growing chillies is that they like to have warm feet. The compost temperature should be kept up. Protect the plants from frost and water from a can that has been left in the greenhouse and is warm. Feed weekly with general-purpose fertiliser (I use tomato feed).

TOP TIP

HANDLING SEEDLINGS

When potting on, handle the plant only by the leaves, never the stem, and ease it out of its compost and into a new home using a dibber or a pencil.

Keeping the plants warm brings with it the possibility of fungal diseases. This can be avoided by ensuring they are well ventilated. Also, avoid water stress. Watering the plants sporadically and allowing them to wilt damages the tissues and creates an opportunity for fungal infection. Try not to have too many plants on the same bench.

Aphids like chillies and should be removed because they introduce viral diseases, as well as promoting fungal disease. When an aphid punctures the plant it ferrets around inside until it finds the phloem tubes, which are full of sugar and under pressure. The liquid gushes into the insect and out its back end. Consequently the plant is covered in its own sap and fungi grow on this. Use your favourite method of removing greenfly and blackfly, but do not let them build up on the plant.

CAPSICUMS

Capsicums are very easy to grow. Treat them like chillies and limit them to six fruits per plant. They grow best in pots and are ideal for the kitchen windowsill too!

Varieties

To my mind, unless you are going to be a chilli aficionado there are only a couple of varieties worth growing for all-round use.

'Jalapeño Hercules': A robust-growing variety that produces large, smooth, green fruits, which ripen to an intense bright red. Very reliable and well suited to the UK's short growing season. This is a good all-round chilli and not too hot – around 3,000 Scoville Heat Units, which is nearly 200-times 'cooler' than Habañeros. Excellent for eating raw, incorporating into salsas, using in soups and stews, or stuffing with cheese and roasting.

'Numex Suave Orange': All the classic smoky flavour of a Habañero chilli with none of the heat. This is a must-have chilli for chilli-lovers, chilli-haters and keen chefs – everyone in fact! So many people miss out on the distinct flavours of different chillies because their taste buds are zapped by the heat, but with 'Suave Orange' everyone will be able to experience these delicate flavours.

Melons

If you have a polytunnel you can grow melons quite easily. They like rich soil and you need to grow them in the ground rather than in a bag if you are to be successful with them.

Sowing

- Buy specific seeds and choose early varieties, they will do better.
- Sow two seeds per 8cm (3in) pot at a temperature of around 20°C and water in.
- Discard the slowest growing plants and then grow the seedling until it has about three leaves.
- Plant out into its final growing position.
- When the plant has about five leaves, prick out the growing point. The plant will then produce four or five laterals, each of which will bear a melon.
- Melons produce two kinds of flower, male and female. The female ones have melons behind the flower. Pull off male flowers and use them to pollinate the female ones.
- Sometimes you will get two melons on a lateral branch, if so, remove the smallest.
- From now on it is a matter of feeding (use tomato feed) and watering, just like tomatoes.
- Melons are ripe when you can smell them – you will notice the fragrance.

Varieties

I have had success with 'Blenheim Orange' and 'Castella'. The former is a good all-rounder and it is easy to grow, while the latter one is a big fruit, juicy and lovely.

Peaches, nectarines and apricots

Peaches, nectarines and apricots all do well in polytunnels. They grow tall if left to their own devices, and even if you have them on dwarfing rootstocks they will still reach to the top of the polytunnel, so you will have some pruning to do. They are probably best trained as espaliers.

If you grow them in containers, they can spend the warmest days outside on the plot, but use at least a 75cm (30in) pot and change the compost as often as possible without damaging the roots. In the winter keep the plants frost-free but cool – as cool as possible.

Water and feed weekly during the growing season and do not allow too many fruits to form per branch or they will be weighed down.

Pruning

I have grown peaches, nectarines and apricots against a wall and inside a tunnel and I have to say they are best trained against a wall in an espalier or a fan. This keeps the height

down and provides a useful guide for pruning. In December, cut out a third of the growth, dead wood, crossing wood and so on.

Pests

If grown outside these fruits can get peach leaf curl, but not in the tunnel. Keeping the plants dry seems to be enough to keep the pests at bay. Red spider mite and aphids can also be a problem, for which you can take your pick of the numerous solutions.

Passion flower

Passiflora edulis is a fast-growing, climbing shrub that will reach 5m (16ft) if allowed. It holds itself in place by means of tendrils, and flowers in this country from June to August.

Passion flower will grow on any soil as long as it is well drained and fairly nutrient rich. But it will not tolerate shade and to encourage it to fruit it needs to be grown in a tunnel, although it will grow outside quite successfully in the south of Britain.

The varieties with edible fruit include *P. edulis*, *P. incarnata* and *P. vitifolia*. You can buy seeds quite readily in the UK, and they need to be sown under heat in late winter; January is a good time. Some growers advise soaking the seeds. They germinate in a month and grow quickly. By June they can be transplanted to their growing position in the tunnel. A framework of wires against the end wall is a good place, so long as it is sunny.

Each spring give the plant a good mulch of compost and feed during the summer (tomato feed is as good as any). When the fruits fall off the plant they are ripe. You can cut the branches back once the plant threatens to hit the roof.

Citrus fruits

Members of the citrus family – oranges, lemons, limes, grapefruits – are prized for their flavoursome fruits and vitamin C content. In fact, they contain no more vitamin C than most other plants, but this notion has remained since Georgian times when they were used at sea to ward off scurvy.

When you think of citrus fruit, oranges and lemons immediately spring to mind, but it is possible to grow others in the UK. Clementines, mandarins, satsumas, grapefruits, kumquats and limes, as well as bergamot – so you can make your own Earl Grey tea – all do well over here.

Growing conditions

■ All citrus plants can be easily grown in the UK as long as you provide a frost-free environment in the winter months. Cold, wind and rain combine to make these plants miserable and they need to be brought inside in the autumn. They are tolerant of cold down to around 5°C, so an unheated polytunnel is the best. Try to keep them in the sunniest spot, not necessarily for the heat it brings but because they will prefer it.

Just because it is winter does not mean that citrus plants are going to 'sleep'. In fact, they actively grow during this period and most of them flower in the winter. An orange in flower on Christmas day is a lovely sight.

■ In order to bring them in during the winter, these plants need to be grown in pots. For preference, a large terracotta pot is best because it is porous and provides an amount of air to the roots. In addition, it will more readily allow for the evaporation of water and store heat for longer than a plastic equivalent. As far as size is concerned, a 60cm (24in) pot for a small citrus tree will be perfectly adequate. Fill the pot with a soil-based compost (John Innes No. 2) and incorporate some sand into the mix, up to 25%.

■ Citrus plants generally need the same regime when it comes to watering and feeding. They do not like to stand in wet conditions, but do enjoy moisture. However, take care not to over-water; simply make sure the soil is slightly moist, and that the pots are positively free-draining.

Use a good quality general fertiliser (ensuring that it has all the necessary trace elements) at least once a month – possibly once a fortnight in the spring. Some people use winter-feed and a separate summer feed. But, as long as you use a good quality, all-round fertiliser, this expense is not necessary in my view. Feed less in the winter, just once a month or so.

Re-potting and pruning

This is best done in the spring. Trim your plant just above a fat, lush-looking bud, so the tree takes on a good, roundish shape and remains at the appropriate height for your tunnel.

Re-pot yearly into the next size up. Take the opportunity to add some slow-release fertiliser and fresh, well-draining compost. Gently remove some of the soil and ensure there is plenty of crockery in the bottom of the new pot for drainage. Add new compost/sand mixture and firm well in. Give a good watering, and keep the plant out of draughts/wind for a few days.

Pests and problems

All citrus plants suffer from the same group of pests: aphids, red spider mite and scale insects. A weekly wash with soft soap will keep most of these in check. They drop their leaves regularly in the winter, but should not lose more than a third. Any evidence of yellowing leaves could be due to over-watering, lack of nutrients, low temperatures or insufficient sunlight.

Keep plants well ventilated but out of strong draughts to avoid botrytis and other fungal infections.

PROPAGATING CITRUS FRUITS

Most citrus plants will grow readily from fresh seed, but will take around a decade to flower and fruit, sometimes two. Plants can be grown by taking hardwood cuttings in the autumn; around half will 'take' and, after a couple of years, the trees might produce fruit.

Citrus plants bought from garden centres and nurseries are grafted on to specialised rootstocks, and the vigour that this ensures means that they will grow to their full height very quickly.

Most plants are propagated by budding; where a single bud is grafted on to a rootstock/scion combination.

ZEST FOR CITRUS

Oranges

Every navel orange is a descendant of a single mutant tree found in the early 19th century in Brazil. It was budded and the small plants sent around the world. They are a very heavy fruit and, consequently, the trees need to be large to take their weight. The fruits are seedless and have a small 'baby' fruit inside them.

Blanco oranges are smaller and can be borne on smaller trees. Most fruits can be harvested in November and December.

Grapefruits

Grapefruits first appeared in the West Indies – another mutation – in 1750, and were transported as buds all around the world. They were particularly prized by rich English landowners who grew them in hot houses, even though they can be taken outside in the summer. The plants are larger than oranges, and bear larger fruits. Otherwise they can be treated in exactly the same way.

Kumquats

This is a fast-growing tree and the fruits can be eaten whole. They are also supposed to be good pickled in brandy. They grow to be quite large and, for this reason, are kept in a single position.

Clementines and satsumas

These plants ripen around Christmas, most being ready after November. They can be kept quite small, even though they are vigorous plants. Annual trimming keeps them in check, but you can grow them up a wall or as a large bush.

Nothing is more exciting than citrus fruit growing indoors.

TOP TIP

CITRUS SUCCESS

Whichever citrus plant you want to grow, they're easy as long as you follow the rules:

■ **Keep plants cool but frost-free in winter – minimum 5°C**

■ **Water freely, but ensure good, free-draining**

■ **Feed regularly in the summer, less so in winter**

■ **Prune and re-pot in spring**

Limes and limequats

Limes tend to be easy to grow and can be restricted to a reasonably small tree of about 1.7m (5½ft) high. There are a number of varieties and each grows well in the UK – some turning yellow when ripening. A limequat is a cross between a lime and a kumquat. You can eat the whole fruit, and it tastes like a lime.

INSIDE OUT

All plants grown outside can be grown inside. It is a matter of choice and available space versus the prevailing weather. For most of us the weather means that sweet corn is as well grown inside early, then outside later. In the far north you might want to grow it inside all the year round.

You can fill in spaces all over the polytunnel, at any time of the year, with radishes, lettuces, cabbages and even Christmas potatoes (*see A to Z of vegetables, page 108*).

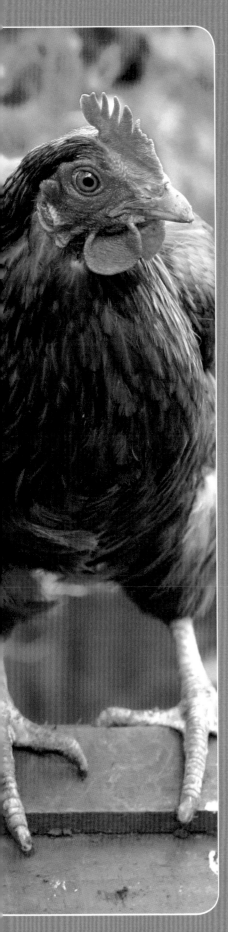

LIVESTOCK

Hens on the allotment offer so much more than just eggs! They bring you manure, and a whole lot of fun.

Living the good life is one of the major reasons why people get allotments. Of course, rows of carrots lead on to dreams of hens, bees and much more. In days of austerity, such as during the Second World War, allotments were used to provide all kinds of life's requirements. However, days of plenty have all but conspired to spoil the fun.

Note: This chapter is not a complete guide to keeping livestock on allotments. You should refer to other literature and get advice, both as a committee and individuals. For comprehensive information on keeping chickens – see the Haynes *Chicken Manual*.

Until very recently it was all but illegal to keep livestock on allotments, though few local authorities actually passed byelaws against keeping livestock. There are some legal hurdles that might prevent certain animals from being kept –

goats, pigs, sheep and cattle need a holding number from the government before you can keep them. You will not be allocated a holding number if the officials deem the allotments unsuitable.

Another point to remember is that goats, in order to look after them properly, need space, as do sheep and pigs. An allotment plot will not provide enough space to keep them disease free. Parasites build up in the soil and the animals need to be moved around, which takes up more room. As waiting lists grow for allotments, one wonders if this is good use of the resources we have.

For the majority of allotments, livestock means rabbits, hens and bees. To be honest, keeping rabbits for food purposes on allotments is probably not going to be acceptable for many people, and is probably best avoided. You are allowed to kill rabbits for food, singly, by neck dislocation, just like hens, but you are not allowed to do it in front of the animals or children.

That said, most people keep hens for fun and eggs, and many a hen on an allotments site lives in conditions better than many people. We will look at keeping hens and bees on allotments.

Keeping hens

There are a number of things to bear in mind when keeping hens on allotments, some for animal welfare reasons, some for public health reasons.

Be aware that escaped hens will nibble more or less anything.

Where to put the henhouse

Whether you allow hens in restricted areas or on individual allotments is a matter of debate. If hens are kept on soil or grass (which will quickly become mud in the winter), they should be put onto new pasture every three months. This is to reduce the impact of the build-up of parasites in the soil. If they are kept on concrete or paving, this is not so important, but the area should be washed regularly, and the poo removed.

It is a good idea to keep the hens as far away from houses as possible to reduce the nuisance from smells and noise.

No cockerels

Cockerels can be noisy – especially where they can see other cockerels – and the source of a lot of irritation for neighbours, particularly at 3am in the summer! You do not need to keep cockerels for the hen's welfare, and generally they get on perfectly well without them. Hens only make a mild chuckle and sometimes a little more when laying, but never enough to disturb anyone.

Feed storage

It is not the hens that attract rats, but their feed, which should be kept locked in a separate shed or container. Only the needs of the day or couple of days should ever be held at the pen and any spillages (if your hens are as messy as mine) should be cleaned up. Cleanliness is the best protection from rats.

There are so many different types of hen house – from plastic to homemade.

Space

You should allow a run with at least 1sq m (1sq yard) per bird, preferably 2sq m. Bear in mind the importance of removing poo, which can be composted. Perhaps the best reason for keeping hens is the manure: a bird will plop every 5 to 10 minutes and you do get a lot of it!

Housing

There are many designs of hutch on the market, and in true allotment tradition, you see mostly modified sheds. To avoid problems of birds eating other plot-holder's crops, insist on good quality fencing, and that the bird's wings are clipped.

Inside, the hut should have bedding – mostly to mop up the poo. Suitable materials include chippings or wood, but you can use straw or shredded paper. You will always find people who say you cannot use this or that, and some people say you should not use straw because some birds are allergic to it. However, in 30 years of keeping hens I have never found any problems, and it is a great insulator.

The hutch should have a perch for the birds, and plenty of space for them to roost without competition from other birds.

Nest boxes are inviting places for the birds to lay, and if you make a little nest of your favourite bedding material, the birds will recognise what they are and lay in them. The nest boxes need to be just big enough for a hen to fit in.

Check the inside of the hutch for red mites on a regular basis every week and deal with what you find in there. You can use powder and a blowtorch – which works well. Powder should be used monthly to prevent infestations from building up. The mites crawl onto the hen's legs at night and suck their blood.

Evidence of intruders

Look all around the hut for holes nibbled by rats, and droppings other than hen droppings. These are evidence of rats and mice. Reinforce any holes with metal if you can manage it, and think about where the rats are coming from. If you can lift the hut off the ground, then they will not be able to congregate beneath. Be sure you clear away food spillages, and consider taking the food out each evening.

Feeding

It is often wrongly suggested that hens will live happily from scraps. They will not. The basic diet of a chicken is grain, modified grain at that. Layers pellets or layers mash contains the balanced diet a chicken needs, and all other foods are supplements.

Hens should be allowed to eat solely from layers rations (pellets or mash) in the morning and only then be given extras. Hens are not greedy, and will not eat again until they are ready. If they constantly fill up on less nutritious food (bread, salad or whatever), they might not get a balanced diet even if layers pellets are available for them.

Feeders keep the food in one place.

If your hens' poo is runny and does not form a good solid mass, there might be too much protein in the mix. You can change to a lower mix; most pellets are 16% protein, but you can find suppliers that offer 15%.

Hens need a good supply of grit for grinding their food and for making shells on the eggs. This is supplied in broken shell, which they eat.

They need a good supply of clean water, and it is here you will find hens messy. They move their food about, and can dirty their water supplies.

Feeders

Feed suppliers around the country and on the Internet offer a range of poultry feeders and drinkers. Bowl type troughs offer easy access, but can be messy, particularly if your birds are used to eating with a swipe of the head.

How much time is involved?

Hens need daily attention to ensure there are no problems (if, for example, a hen dies and you don't notice it, you can be certain someone else will). You need to ensure that they have sufficient food and water, that runs are secure, eggs are collected and bedding is tidy and unspoiled. This takes about 10 minutes a day.

Then you have to ensure they are safely locked away for the night and that Mr Fox and his friends do not have access to the hens. Add to this the weekly clean-out and repairs and you will probably spend a couple of hours a week with your birds.

Handling hens

Talking to your hens and picking them up is not a sign of madness, but good hen management. If you have a sick hen that needs attention, having to chase it around the run is going to add to its stress. If they are used to being handled, gently but firmly, they will be all the easier to deal with, and should you have to kill the bird because it is so poorly, it will not be worried about being picked up.

Sick hens

There are many reasons for hens becoming sick. You should look out for:
- Scales on the legs – could be a mite problem
- Pecking at the anus – could be mites or bullying
- Bloody or constantly runny poo – could be worms
- Dull comb and wattles – could be any kind of infection in older birds
- Discharge from the nose – could be a viral or other infection
- Scruffy lonely bird – could be bullying or infection.

This is not a treatise on bird diseases, you will find plenty of reference sources on the Internet. Remember, you are not allowed to treat birds by law, you must seek veterinary advice if you suspect a bird is ill. However, you can take preventative action, which includes:

ACV Apple cider vinegar is a great tonic for birds, and 100ml (3.4fl oz) diluted in 5 litres (1gal) of water once a month is enough to help to keep them healthy. It is amazing how this tends to make the birds perky and shine.

Worming This should be done every three months. You simply pour the appropriate powder onto their food. Most worms can be dealt with, but cases of lung worm might need veterinary assistance.

Cleaning Clear away debris, kill red mites as described above, and look out for bullying. A lonely bird that is not eating well is often pecked at and has blood drawn from wounds. As soon as the other birds taste blood from another they rarely leave it alone, and the only option is separation.

What kind of birds should I choose?

This is no easy answer. The main reason why people keep hens is usually quite personal – some want pretty birds, some want birds to eat, some want egg layers.

The best hens to keep, in most cases, are those designed for the egg production, otherwise known as Little Brown Jobbies, or LBJs. They include the Warren type of bird. The reason for this is they rarely fight, they rarely if ever go broody and are usually healthy.

How many birds?

You should get at least three birds. Hens are social animals, and if one happens to die, it is cruel to keep a single bird alone. Do not mix new ex-battery hens and established birds.

Ex-battery hens are often in good health, but they may not live as long as other hens – so keep at least three.

If you have to introduce any birds to an existing flock, a good idea is to arrange their coops so they can see each other but cannot gain access to each other. It takes about a week for them to get used to other hens, and you can join them unless there have been altercations at the fence. Be aware how the hens react to each other before and after joining and you will get an idea of how safe they are.

EX-BATTERY HENS

A number of charities give away ex-battery hens, and there are good reasons for having them. Contrary to popular myth, ex-battery hens are mostly very healthy birds. They have had all kinds of treatments to prove it, too. Sure, they are often missing feathers, but they soon colour up and do very well.

If you go for battery hens, they need:

- Quiet and no stress, especially from other birds.
- To sleep flat on the floor, not on a perch, as their muscles will not be up to gripping at first.
- Good food – you can buy specially formulated rations – and no extras to start with.

New beekeepers inspecting hives.

Keeping bees

This is not the place to learn how to keep bees, though some of what follows will give the reader an idea of some of the important points. People new to beekeeping should go on a recognised course, be a member of their local beekeeping association and have a mentor.

The committee
There are some things to bear in mind before you allow bees on the allotment. It is not a bad idea to have a relationship with your local beekeeping association, who will advise you

about where to position the bees. You will also need to be a member of the association – at least the individual beekeepers will – in order to obtain bee insurance against people being stung and against loss due to certain diseases.

Gentle bees
- Choose bees that are gentle. There are many varieties and sub species of bee. If the bees go for you or follow you if you walk near them, or directly attack you, you need gentler bees. Your local bee inspector will be able to point you in the direction of a supply of gentle bees.
- Make sure the bees are 'diluted' by trees and distance before they reach nearby houses.
- Site the bees away from public thoroughfares, bus stops and schools.
- Put a fence around the hives so the bees have to fly upwards and are well above head height before flying off to forage.

Benefits of beekeeping
You can sell honey – people will pay considerably for a jar of local honey. A couple of hives could easily make £500 for the allotment site. Pollinated crops have improved yields just because of the bees. Then there are other products, such as wax, propolis and, above all, the interest of keeping bees.

Note: This chapter is not a complete guide to keeping livestock on allotments. You should refer to other literature and get advice, both as a committee and individuals. For comprehensive information on keeping bees – see the Haynes Bee Manual.

Haynes
Bee
Manual
The complete step-by-step guide to keeping bees

Claire & Adrian Waring
Foreword by Bill Turnbull

A super frame full of honey.

The kit

You will need a lot of kit, and like most hobbies, it is always expensive.

Bee suit This protects you from stings, especially in the face. The veil should be a double one and the zips should be strong.

Gauntlets Regardless of what macho beekeepers say, gauntlets keep your hands safe. When you get used to beekeeping and handling bees you can probably progress to rubber gloves.

Hives It is probably best to start with a National hive, and become used to making frames and keeping bees in this format. A good one will cost about £200 at current prices. You need to have the ability to house a spare hive at any moment, consequently you might need two hives for one colony, five for three colonies and so on.

A simple hive consists of:

- base
- varroa floor
- brood box
- queen excluder
- at least two super boxes
- crown board and a lid
- frames with foundation beeswax for each box, usually 11 per box.

Smoker Bees evolved in a woodland environment and consequently have a mechanism for dealing with fire. When they detect smoke they rush into the colony stores to fill up with honey, then they find it more difficult to sting. More than that, they do not like smoke and will move away from it. Smoking bees controls them, makes them easier to deal with and keeps them from attacking you in the hive.

Hive tool This is a simple knife with a lever built into the design. It is used for scraping wax, levering frames and prizing glued boxes apart – bees love to glue everything together.

Feeder Bees need to be fed at many times during the year, especially if the nectar flow is disturbed, when bees cannot forage (in winter) and when you have taken honey. Bees are fed ordinary sugar syrup of differing strengths depending on the time of the year and the needs of the bees.

Bee year

Much of the winter is spent making sure the bees remain alive and keeping them fed. During the winter they are given candy, and at other times of the year syrup. As the spring warms up the hive, the queen starts to lay and the bees start to fly to forage for food – nectar and pollen.

The number of bees in a hive increases to 30,000 or more in the height of the summer. The queen is trapped in the brood area, where she lays eggs with a special grille called a queen excluder. This keeps her from laying eggs in the higher (super) boxes, which will contain just honey, some of which we shall take.

Varroa

The art of beekeeping has become the science of maintaining low numbers of varroa mites. This is done by various applications of natural oils at specific times of the year, by having a varroa floor so that mites can fall out of the hive, and a number of other treatments and mechanisms.

A full kit for beekeeping is an expensive purchase.

A YEAR ON THE ALLOTMENT

At the height of summer, the allotment is full and colourful.

The jobs outlined below from month to month are only a guide gleaned from notes I have collected over the years. There is plenty of leeway in the garden, especially when it comes to planting and growing. There is hardly anything that will not produce a decent crop in the garden if planted too late. However, you can plant too early.

Every gardener knows the temptation to get plants in the ground, and the abject disaster of trying too soon, of having seedlings you know are never going to survive, and plants in the ground you cannot sustain. Perhaps the best way to maintain a good regime on the plot is to copy what some of the older gardeners do, the members who have been doing it for years. You can encourage yourself by trying to grow better crops if you like, but on the whole it is best to follow their lead.

Do not try to force the crops into too early or too late a cropping period – you might get away with it once or twice, but generally the result is disease. Immunity in plants stretches only within a few weeks of their season. If you put a plant under stress by growing it too fast, or making it grow too far beyond its season, often you cause its natural immunity to suffer.

You can, using a greenhouse or a polytunnel, make the season stretch maybe a month or six weeks either side of the norm. You could have potatoes in a tunnel in the ground in February, and have a separate crop at Christmas. If you have a cloche you might extend the growing season by a few weeks, but by far the best use of these tools in the garden is the production of high-class produce, not battered by the elements.

Carrots in tubes – are they covered? They certainly are protected.

Different forms of covered gardening – notice the fleece triangle.

JANUARY

January is a time of sowing, watching the weather, cleaning, preparing and planning. The allotment shed or clubhouse is often the last refuge on snowy and frosty days. Personally I find the snowy allotment a great attraction. Mug of tea in hand, I experience a peace that is simply amazing when it comes to sitting in the shed, watching nature doing her work under a white blanket.

But there is a lot to do too! Possibly the most important thing is to check the way the plants are secure in the ground. Any loose ones will be rocked out of the soil in strong winds, so heel them in.

Sowing
Beets and salad leaves: continue to sow, even in the coldest weeks.

Chives

Leeks

Onions

Shallots

Tomatoes: towards the end of the month start tomatoes off ready for inside and outside.

Growing
- Force rhubarb by putting a bucket over the plant. Mulch well-rotted manure and then straw onto rhubarb crowns – around 30cm (12in) deep to give them an extra boost.
- Order seed potatoes and start the process of chitting.
- You can still plant bare-rooted fruit trees and fruit canes.

Maintenance
- Study the seed catalogues and plan your plot. Order seeds.
- Remember to lag and protect any outside water pipes against the cold.
- Don't forget to feed the birds. Fat balls are the highest energy feeds for many birds, oily seeds for others. Take care to wash the feeders and do not leave stale food about.
- Clean out cold frames and greenhouses.
- Deal with moss on paths and between glass in greenhouses.
- A good thick mulch of well-rotted manure on dug potato beds will ensure a great crop.
- Why not compost all your Christmas paper and cardboard from the mountain of presents?
- Sharpen and clean all your tools ready for the hard work of spring.
- If you have bees, treat for varroa with oxalic acid.
- Move hens to new ground at least every three months, or if on concrete, give the slabs a good clean.

Pests and other problems
January is a good time to spray the fruit trees with an organic winter wash against woolly aphids and other insect pests.

FEBRUARY

This month can be a long one despite being the shortest. Freezing, dark winters are miserable. But when the winters are mild, you will find yourself having to trim back the roses because they are growing too quickly. So February is a time for making decisions.

It is possible to predict hard and soft winters. The sun works on an 11-year cycle, so you get a few hard years together and then a few years of average cold temperatures and then a few of relative warmth.

Sowing

Aubergines: sow indoors later in the month for a crop in June.

Beets and salad leaves: continue to sow, even in the coldest weeks.

Peppers: sow under heat.

Tomatoes: you can still sow tomatoes ready for inside and outside growing.

Growing

■ Plant out shallots towards the end of the month.
■ You should be chitting your potatoes.
■ Last chance to plant bare-rooted fruit trees.
■ Last chance to plant garlic.
■ Check up on broad beans planted last October, and Japanese onions.
■ By now, parsnips will be perfect.
■ Continue to harvest leeks.

A chitted potato.

Maintenance

■ February is a great month for working on paths and allotment-wide projects, including fencing, digging out foundations in mild weeks, trying to maintain water supplies, and for jobs inside, like painting the clubhouse.
■ If you are having a show this season, it is a good time to get the schedules out to everyone and to allot jobs for other various events during the year.
■ The spring newsletter can be started now. Include what to do in spring, events you have planned, what is available in the shop. Why not include a survey about an aspect of allotment life on your site, and ask members for their stories, such as what are they growing and how the winter has gone for them.
■ If you have communal hens, give their coop a clean and renew the litter.
■ Empty your water butts, clean them and make sure the lids work properly.
■ Dig over your potato, carrot and onion beds, and add plenty of well-rotted organic material.
■ Cover soil that has been dug so it can warm up ready for planting.
■ Sharpen and clean all your tools ready for spring. Ensure the Rotavator is working; if you have a communal one, it will be in great demand, so make sure it is in good order.

Pests and other problems

Insects will be waking up towards the end of the month. Spray fruit trees with organic insecticide. Buy in horticultural fleece, or at least check the old for rips.

MARCH

Gardeners everywhere are developing itchy feet and fingers, hoping to get everything in the ground. Be patient, it is much better to sow later rather than early. A couple of days of frost can easily destroy all your good work. Since St Patrick's Day (17 March) is the traditional time to plant first early potatoes, give the bed a quick dig over.

Sowing

UNDER COVER
Cabbage: 'January King'
French beans: in 8cm (3in) pots

OUTDOORS
Beetroot: 'Boltardy'
Broad beans: 'Express'
Brussels sprouts
Carrots (maincrop)
Cauliflowers: 'All Year Round'
Peas
Spinach
Turnips

Planting

OUTDOORS
- First early potatoes: 'Home Guard', 'Accord', 'Maris Peer', 'Swift'
- Maincrop Potatoes: 'Picasso', 'Desiree'
- Onion sets: 'Sturon'

Onion sets pushing themselves through the earth.

Pests and other problems

- **Young slugs and snails** are in need of food and will go to extraordinary lengths to get it, bypassing what looks like good food and going straight for your tasty seedlings. All kinds of protection from eggshells to pellets are available, but it is too cold for biological measures.
- **Birds and mice** Lay netting, especially against pigeons, and try to cover all round the plants to soil level – mice are hungry too.
- **Damping off** Seedlings that are too wet in an over-humid, heated greenhouse can get fungal problems. Try to maintain a good temperature with some periods of ventilation.
- **Carrot root fly** If you have planted 'Nantes Early' then you will have to cover with fleece to protect from the first flyings of carrot root fly.
- **Frosts** Protect fruit blossom from heavy frosts – spraying with water can help.

Maintenance

- Mulch fruit trees with 15cm (6in) of compost.
- Open cold frames for 30 minutes to ventilate them on warm days.
- Turn your compost over – most people go from one frame to another. A cold day keeps you fresh as this is hard work.
- Check the water is working around the plots and look for leaks.
- March is a great month for a general clean-up day, when all the members give the site a spring clean.

APRIL

The garden is racing towards normality, but remember, there is still a chance of a frost, so be ready to protect plants. April is an awkward month: often wet, often cold, often dry, often hot and sunny, often all the year's weather in a single day.

Sowing

UNDER COVER

Broccoli: 'Belstar F1' or 'Boltardy'. Protect from frost before planting out in late May.

French bean: 'Mantra' is an excellent variety for a great crop.

Runner bean: 'Scarlet Emperor' is my favourite. Sow in pots and transplant when 10cm (4in) tall.

Summer cauliflower: 'Mayflower', 'Snow Crown', 'All the year round'.

Summer Cabbage: 'Durham Early' is a good one to start now. Sow in modules and thin to a single plant. Plant out in a well-limed hole in late May.

Sweetcorn: 'Lark' or 'Honey Bantam'. Sow two seeds per pot in a heated greenhouse, at 15°C. Transplant in June into blocks for best pollination.

Tomatoes: there is still time to sow tomatoes for indoor or outdoor varieties.

Sowing outdoors for beans is possible.

OUTSIDE:

Beetroot: 'Solo' or 'Boltardy' are great ones to grow. Sow every fortnight for a constant crop.

Brussels sprouts

Carrots: 'Nantes' varieties and 'Chantenay' do well sown this month.

Lettuce: sow the 'Iceberg' types and a row of 'Little Gem', and continue sowing through the summer. Try the leafier varieties later in June.

Maincrop onions: 'Ailsa Craig' sown in a fine bed does well, but consider sets.

Maincrop peas: 'Kelvedon Wonder' or 'Feltham First'. Sow in drills, 6cm (2in) deep, 30cm (12in) apart.

Shallots: I have had good results from 'Atlantic'. 'White Lisbon' sown in a finely hoed bed every two weeks will give salad onions right through the summer. Try them in containers too.

Planting

OUTDOORS

Maincrop potatoes: there is still time to get them in the ground.

Start to prick out brassica seedlings.

Using a garden line and a measure makes the best use of space.

Onion sets: 'Sturon' is the main variety and is still going strong.

Perpetual strawberries: the main varieties are planted in the autumn, but 'Mae' and 'Sweet Temptation' can go in now.

Pests and other problems

- **Aphids** At the end of April the first aphids start to appear. You can spray against them or use the finger and thumb method.
- **Birds** Netting is the best protection.
- **Pea moth** Normally appears from May to July, but has been coming earlier in some areas. The pea moth will lay eggs that produce grubs that burrow through the peas. A good net is the best idea.
- **Slugs and snails** The not so small army of molluscs are abroad, but it is still too cold to use biological methods.

Maintenance

- Ventilate greenhouses and polytunnels on warm days, and don't forget cold frames.
- Make home-made fertilisers – fill an old pillowcase with manure, tie a knot in it, and drop it in the water butt for liquid feeds.
- Prepare compost and sterilise over a fire if necessary.
- Stock the shop with growbags, fertiliser and all the various items people will need.
- Deliver the spring newsletter.
- Collect orders for manure and place order.
- Turn communal compost.
- Collect items for the spring committee meeting.

MAY

The gardens change in May. The swifts appear, the seedlings become plants and yet there is still time to get jobs done. There might just be a frost in May. I have been on the plot in June covered in snow, so this month is a delicate one. It might be glorious weather. Who knows?

May is a time for hardening off plants, leaving them outside during the day and taking them indoors for the night as a protection against frost, so that you can start the job of planting out at the end of the month and into June.

Sowing

OUTDOORS

Beans of all kinds: you may have started some in pots indoors earlier in the year, but if not, you can sow them in their beds this month.

Carrots

Peas

Radishes

Salads: keep sowing your salad leaves.

Squashes: if you want a good Halloween pumpkin or other squashes, then sow them in rich soil in late May.

Sweetcorn: in southern England you can sow sweetcorn into soil previously warmed by using black plastic.

Sunflowers: great to plant outside. As well as looking good, they are super for feeding to hens once the seeds are mature.

Turnips

Winter cabbages: in a seedbed.

Early cabbages on their way in May.

Planting

- Continue to plant main crop potatoes.
- Plant out summer cabbages and other brassicas.
- Plant out celery and any beans grown in pots.

Harvest

Among the salads, it is time to harvest asparagus.

Pests and other problems

Aphids including blackfly on beans. You can spray them or use the finger and thumb method.

Mice eating peas and beans – netting is the best option.

Slugs and snails Use biological methods of control.

Maintenance

- Hoe out weeds all over the plot.
- Continue preparing compost and give leaf mould a turn with the fork to aerate it.
- Assess the water situation – do you need a top-up?
- Worm chickens.
- Begin swarm regime for bees and count varroa.
- Start the summer newsletter.
- Continue preparations for show.
- Clean tools in tool store.
- Collect information and items for summer committee meeting
- Have a general inspection of the allotments, concentrating on communal areas.

As the plants grow, so does the wildlife that feeds on them.

JUNE

At last the garden looks like a garden. A good time for a competition. The plants are not yet mature in June, so there are several that need caring for. Yes, you can still plant potatoes!

Sowing

CONTINUE TO SOW THE FOLLOWING PLANTS

INDOORS
Courgettes
French beans
Lettuces
Pak Choi
Peas
Radishes
Salad onions
Summer cabbage
Sweetcorn
Tomatoes

SOW OUTDOORS
Beetroot
Brussels sprouts
Carrots
Lettuce
Maincrop onions
Maincrop peas
Spring onions

Planting

Outdoors, you can still plant potatoes and they are often best. You can make a second planting of first earlies, giving a crop in September.

Indeed, some pundits predict the demise of maincrop potatoes because they take a long time in the ground, and then they have to be stored, often without success.

Growing

■ Feed all your container-grown fruit.
■ Indoor tomatoes will need to be put into final growing positions.
■ Start weekly feeding regime for tomatoes and peppers.

Harvest

Beets and kales
Broccoli
Cauliflower
Salads
Wintered onions
Strawberries are out in force and the best time to harvest them is from now and throughout the summer.

Over-wintered onions will be ready.

Beat the farmers! Grow your own strawberries for early June.

Ventilate

On warm days open up your cold frames, greenhouses and polytunnels to give the hardening-off seedlings air. Close them at night.

Pests and other problems

Aphids In greenhouses, try some ladybird larvae to control aphids – the enclosed areas mean you won't lose them to next door!

Birds Use good netting.

Fungal infections Watch out for fungal infections, both indoors and out. Early blight is not so bad on potatoes and tomatoes, just destroy affected parts.

Pea moth Use good netting.

Young slugs and snails Nematodes are useful now the soil has warmed up.

Maintenance

■ Clean, sharpen and oil spades and forks after the spring digging.
■ Oil and clean the Rotavator.
■ Consider placing fleece around the plot to keep insects off the produce and whitewashing the greenhouse.

JULY

Sometime in July you need to sit back and admire your garden, which is generally at its peak before all the fruits and crops start to come in.

Sowing

Carrots
Chicory
Chinese brassicas
Japanese onions Can be sown between now and the end of August
Lettuce
Salad onions Keep on sowing until August/September
Turnips

Harvest

It should be fairly obvious what you can harvest – almost everything. When it comes to taking fruit and veg from the garden, don't wait until the produce is huge because it will be past its best. Small is best! Each plant has an optimum size, so pick it when this is reached. This is particularly true for plants such as cucumbers. The longer you wait for them, the less tasty they will be. Moreover, if you pick them regularly the plant will be encouraged to set more fruit.

You should be enjoying lots of new potatoes. Don't be tempted to compost the vines; collect them together and burn them, spreading the cooled ashes around the garden. This way you reduce the possibility of disease next season.

Ventilate

Water to cool the hot greenhouses and polytunnels, then make sure crops that are susceptible to fungal attack have low humidity by increasing ventilation.

Pests and other problems

Aphids Treat as before.
Birds Use good netting.
Codling moth Spray apple and pear trees with derris.
Fungal infection Treat all fruit against infection.
Pea moth Use good netting.
Potato blight Keep a look out when rain falls following a hot dry spell. Do not venture into the greenhouse after tending potatoes because tomatoes are susceptible.
Slugs and snails Treat as before.

Maintenance

- Keep up on the weeds and make sure you suppress them by mulching all around.
- Any areas of ground not being used after harvest can have green manures sown onto them as they become free.
- Prepare for a committee meeting before the holidays start.
- July is a great time to finalise preparations for fêtes, shows and community days.
- Gather together information for the summer newsletter.

Lilies in bloom make the allotment perfect!

If your compost bin is full, its time to turn it over!

AUGUST

Some years August is a blue-sky month, invariably followed by a hosepipe ban. It is also the holiday month and allotment societies struggle to combine fêtes and shops with people being away. In the garden, everything is racing towards fruition, and we start to think about autumn, harvest and, dare I say it, winter!

Sowing

Chicory
Chinese cabbage: Treat as for spring cabbage (see below) and harvest when you have nice plants with succulent stalks.

Radicchio: This vegetable is really worth growing. You can boil or steam it like spinach, or use it raw and chopped in salads. Sow in a seedbed in drills, thinning to about 30–40cm (12–16in), and treat a little like spring cabbage. It will provide leaves right through the autumn and into the new year.

Spring cabbage: 'Spring Hero F1' is a great variety to sow thinly in a seedbed in drills. Thin out seedlings to about 30cm (12in) between plants (a little more for bigger plants). In early winter they are better cloched.

Turnip
Winter lettuce: 'Winter Gem' is just like 'Little Gem' and you can sow this into winter under cover in a cloche or cold greenhouse.

Growing
- Greenhouse tomatoes should have their leaves removed and watering reduced to promote ripening and, more particularly, to keep the humidity around the plants at a minimum. This is one of the best ways to beat fungal infections.
- Keep an eye on fungal infections on the peppers in the tunnel while they are ripening. You can harvest when they have achieved their full colour.
- Earth up your leeks to blanch the stems and to stop them from rocking about in high winds.
- Similarly, make sure your cabbages and other brassicas are firm in the soil.
- Prune out fruited raspberry canes and trim side shoots of gooseberries.
- Take hardwood cuttings.

Harvest
- Most items sown in the spring onwards can be harvested, including potatoes, summer salads, cabbages and roots (except parsnips). Also harvest honey.
- Move hens to new pasture or treat the ground. This is a good time for a spring clean and to treat hens for worms and red mite.

Maintenance
- When you have harvested a plot or a part of a plot, such as a raised bed, it is best to dig it over, fertilise it and prepare it for the next crop. This might include a green manure, such as clover or field lupins. It could mean a layer of well-rotted manure on the surface of the soil for worms to drag down ready for spring, or a simple covering with black membrane to keep the weeds down. Whichever you choose, get the job done now rather than wait for next year.
- Feed anything that has to bring a crop in the early summer. Asparagus beds, for example, could do with a mulch of good, well-rotted manure.
- When you pull a crop, be sure to get it all out. This applies particularly to potatoes, which will appear in your new beds next year if you have left them in.

Espalier apples, and any other, will be slowly filling now.

SEPTEMBER

The planet turns a corner in its journey around the sun and in the UK we really feel the effects. The tides rise, the rivers fill up and the daylight changes. September is a time for preparation.

Sowing

Continue to sow winter crops.

Salad: rocket, mizuna, lettuce and other salads can all be sown. Sow thinly in a drill a little more densely than spring onions. Keep the drills at least 40cm (16in) apart.

Spring cabbage: sow in drills (a 'scrape' in fine soil 6–8cm/2–3in deep and as long as you wish) at 3cm (1in) apart, then thin down gradually until you have plants at about 40cm (16in) apart.

Spring onions: sow in drills as for spring cabbage. Keep the drills at least 40cm (16in) apart.

Turnips: treat as for spring cabbage.

Growing

- Garlic: don't use shop-bought garlic, buy from the garden centre or dealer. Press a clove at 20cm (8in) intervals into the soil about 3cm (1in) deep.
- Onion sets: over-wintering onion sets (little bulbs not seeds) can be pressed into the soil. Use a dibber to make a hole 1cm (½in) deep and firm them in well otherwise they will throw themselves up again. Space at around 30cm (12in). 'Senshyu' is a good one to buy, treat as other onion sets and try to keep them out of puddles and wet ground.

Herbs in pots need to be moved into a cool greenhouse, and trimmed for winter.

Maintenance

- Store only those crops that are completely perfect and eat the rest. (The harvest and sale of crops at this time gave rise to the feast of Michelmass on 29 September, when the rent was due!)
- Top up or start a new compost heap. Give the heap a turn to aerate it.
- Make a rotting trench for broad beans. Dig about 60cm (24in) deep and half fill it with kitchen (only plant) waste and chopped-up vegetables that are not edible (stalks and the like). Refill the trench. This will be a great place to sow broad beans later.

Pests and other problems

Blight Keep watching for blight, especially on tomatoes (probably much of your potato crop will be harvested by now).

Caterpillars All brassicas, including over-wintering cabbages, are in danger from caterpillars and hibernating insects. Remove any eggs you might find on leaves and watch out for silken areas where they are hibernating. (Please leave one cabbage for the wildlife – it would be wrong to push them to extinction.)

Rust Over-wintering onions and leeks get a rust called *puccinia*. Give them a spray with Bordeaux mixture.

Slugs and snails There are still a lot of slugs and snails around, so trap them, bash them, salt them, squeeze them, eat them (well the birds do!) and do what you do to get rid.

Tasks

- Prepare the autumn newsletter.
- Take notes for another committee meeting.

TOP TIP

CHRISTMAS NEW POTATOES

A bit of an experiment this, but worth a go. We have tried two methods.

1 Lift a potato vine from the soil really carefully and remove all but a couple of tubers. Keep the vine intact and cut back to around 30cm. Place in a large container and keep frost free.

2 Gather some new potatoes that are left over (the earlier the better) and put them in compost in a large bucket. As they grow, fill the container with a little more compost until the plant is over the rim.

OCTOBER

A season of mists and all that. October is a time to roll your sleeves up and do a bit of graft, bringing in your harvest and getting ready for next season.

Sowing

Broad beans: in southern areas you can sow a couple of double rows of broad beans. This will give them a head start before the spring, and especially if they are covered with fleece they will do really well. In the north, grow them in the tunnel or under one of those long plastic cloches. Look out for mice taking them. Sow two rows, 30cm (12in) apart, each seed at 30cm (12in) and then another row 60cm (24in) from that if you want.

Lettuces: sow inside or under cloches – they will still push up enough leaves for a sandwich.

Peas: for an early spring crop.

Turnips: if you keep the soil warm using a cloche you can sow turnips and in the winter you will have some little ball roasters.

Growing

■ You can continue to plant garlic any time between now and the middle of November. Press a clove at 20cm (8in) intervals into the soil about 3cm (1in) deep. Similarly, you can continue planting Japanese onions.

■ Keep your brassicas (cabbages, etc) tidy. Remove yellowing leaves which are a source of fungal problems later on.

Maintenance

■ Lift remaining maincrop potatoes and keep them dry if you are to store them. After several years of disappointment, I now store my potatoes on slatted shelves with plenty of air around them.

■ Top up or start a new compost heap. Give the heap a turn to aerate it. If you use a worm bin then now is a good time to insulate it.

■ Clean out the greenhouse and disinfect your tools with Jeyes Fluid or a similar product and give your greenhouse heaters a good clean to make sure they are working. Hunt out a good supply of paraffin – it may be harder than you think.

■ As you clear crops away, give the soil a good dig over so you are ready for spring. A deep layer of well-rotted manure, left on the surface, will give the worms a chance to feed and incorporate the material into the soil.

As you clear beds of crops, prepare them for their new crops as soon as you can.

Pests and other problems

Caterpillars Continue to look out for caterpillars on cabbages and all brassicas. Remove them with your fingers or spray with something like soft soap if the infestation is bad. You will have a cabbage with an inside like soup if you don't.

Rust is an orange *puccinia* fungus that grows on leeks and other crops and can get worse over the winter *(see September)*. Remove leaves that are affected and perhaps spray with traditional copper fungicide if the disease is bad, though likely as not it will be hard to shift.

Slugs and snails Keep on top of them.

Think about wildlife

Hedgehogs, newts, frogs and toads, as well as many beneficial insects, will all be looking to hibernate at this time of the year, so don't be too tidy in the garden, leave some sticks, leaves, logs and some warm compost for them to spend the winter in safety.

NOVEMBER

Normally the time for slippers, cocoa and autumn fires, but there is too much to do outside for all that.

Sowing

Broad beans, cabbages and lettuces: there is still time to sow these inside or under cloches – or even in the open as long as you protect them in bad weather.
Green manure: grow field beans as a green manure.
Onions: start in small pots indoors to have them ready for planting out in spring. (You have to persevere with germination.)
Peas: sow in early part of the month for a late spring crop.

Growing

■ Garlic: continue planting.
■ Jerusalem artichokes, rhubarb and horseradish can all be planted now. Artichokes and horseradish can be invasive, so choose out-of-the-way sites or prepare to manage them. All enjoy well-drained, rich soil, so work in as much manure or organic matter as you can.

Maintenance

■ To encourage the aeration of the soil by worms, add a layer of chicken manure and perhaps leaf mould and top with a layer of compost. By the spring you will have a perfect bed for potatoes.

Small piles of pots make an over-wintering home for important insects.

Discourage pigeons from using your plot for feed.

■ If you have the space, place a bulk order for manure and leave it to rot down over the winter. If you have a choice, use horse manure for heavy soils, cow for lighter conditions.
■ Take a good long look at your beds. If you have been adding plenty of compost and manure you are making soil. The levels will creep up and you might want to reappraise the way the garden is organised.
■ Still time to clean out the greenhouse, disinfect your tools and check your greenhouse heaters are in working order. If you live near an agricultural merchants then 'udder wash' is by far the cheapest way to disinfect your greenhouse or polytunnel.
■ Bring in delicate plants at night, put them out if the weather is good during the day.
■ After the apple harvest, prune both apples and pears.
■ Prune gooseberries, if you don't have a problem with birds. If you do, then put this off until March otherwise they will steal all the buds. Take any crowded side shoots down to two or three buds, leaving any which are in the right place at full length. When pruning, remember the aim is to have an open centre in each bush, to make it easier to pick the fruit later in the year.

Pests and other problems

Clubroot If you had clubroot give the soil a heavy dressing of lime (one big cupful to every 30sq cm/1sq ft – wear rubber gloves and eye protection). Cover with a good 10cm (4in) of compost if you can.
Dead leaves Remove dead leaves from brassicas to keep infections down and firm-in sprouts with your heel.
Pigeons Net all your appetising crops, including brassicas, salads, late carrots and onions, to protect them from pigeons.

DECEMBER

December is more than just Christmas, so take some time out for the garden because there is a lot to do.

Sowing

Beets, broad beans and salad leaves: continue sowing, even on the coldest weeks.

Onions: sow in trays to transplant later in the spring. Keep them frost-free, maintaining about 12°C.

Peas: in the south you can sow peas later in the month, in sheltered positions. Use a cloche for best results.

Radishes: sow in modules ready to plant out in spring.

Shallots: these should be sown on the shortest day and harvested on the longest. Try one pickled shallot from last year with some mature cheddar as a reminder of why you are doing it.

Growing

- Put well-rotted manure and then straw on rhubarb crowns, about 30cm (12in) deep, to give them an extra boost.
- Early in the month check your new potatoes growing indoors for Christmas, make sure the tubers are well covered so they don't green up.
- To force rhubarb, dig up clumps and put them in a decent pot, preferably ceramic. Cover the pot in a stout box that cuts out the light and trigger the plant's growth by warming it up in a shed or greenhouse.

Maintenance

- A spade dug in December is worth three in March. Dig and incorporate as much organic material as you can – some manure, some compost.
- The brassica patch would do well with a really good application of lime, a spade-full per square metre (square yard). This will help control clubroot.
- Clean up the garden by collecting fallen leaves, old plants, fallen crops, old cabbages and sprouts. Remove anything that is rotting and have a look out for anything that might introduce disease.
- Think about wildlife – leave some 'untidy' bits, piles of sticks, and don't forget to feed the birds!
- Remember to lag and protect any outside water pipes against the cold.

Pests and other problems

Chafer grubs You will see a lot of chafer grubs when you are digging. As a rule of thumb, a healthy soil has both carnivores and herbivores. You don't have to kill every insect you see in the soil, they will eat each other over the coming months.

Whitefly You still get overwintering insect pests – look out for whitefly, especially on sprouts when you pick them on Christmas Morning.

Mulch around rhubarb and fruit trees with well-rotted manure.

Tidy around fallen fruit and debris in the garden.

A TO Z OF VEGETABLES

Nothing, in all the world, is more exciting than wonderful fresh vegetables.

Artichokes

Globe artichokes

Globe artichokes are a magnificent sight on the plot. We eat the thistle-like flowers (chokes) with a dainty sauce, dipped as an aperitif.

They need a sunny spot. Try them at the back of the allotment, or as a statement in the corners. The key is the harvest – leave it until the flower opens and it's too late, they are too tough for anything but compost.

SOIL
Artichokes need very well-draining, rich soil. Dig into the site well-rotted manure and a spade full of grit to make the area water retentive, but not wet.

PLANTING
Artichokes are bought as suckers (root and shoot), which need to be planted into a deep hole. You will see a mark showing where the soil has come up to the shoot and the plant should be buried to this line. Back fill, firm in and water well.

CARE
Feed with a good mulch of rich compost in spring and summer and add about 60g (2oz) per square metre (square yard) of organic fertiliser. In late autumn, cut back the growth to ground level and cover with straw, bark or something to protect the plant from the worst of the weather.

HARVESTING
In the first year, remove any buds that form straight away. You need the plant to build up as much reserves as it can. In the second year, take the flowers when they are tight.

PESTS AND PROBLEMS
Aphids, birds and slugs are the main problems, for which there are all manner of remedies, not every one of which actually works.

Jerusalem artichokes

No relation to globe artichoke. Great flavour, but lots of gas, which is why many single people like them. They are tall plants that will produce a lot of tubers, and they are grown from tubers like potatoes.

SOIL
Dig manure into the soil and plant seed tubes at about 60cm (24in) intervals, in rows 1m (3ft) apart. They can be earthed up and then left to grow.

PLANTING
Plant in March–April as seed tubers, and they will appear above the ground within a few weeks. They grow up to 1.8m (6ft) tall. Keep them slightly moist, never dry, but never wet either.

CARE
Jerusalem artichokes are easy to grow and indeed if you leave a piece in the ground, it grows like mad. It is better to replenish stock year on year rather than allowing it to grow and come again. Apart from having good fertility, it grows for fun.

HARVESTING
When the leaves yellow, cut the plants back and you can dig out the tubers as required.

PESTS AND PROBLEMS
None to speak of – even the slugs don't bother that much.

Asparagus

Asparagus can be something of a pain on a small plot because it occupies the same piece of ground for many years. For this reason you need to be aware of pests building up in the soil, and keep up the fertility without disturbing the plant. It is, in fact, quite easy to grow.

A row of 10–15 plants keeps you in asparagus. The plants die back to soil level in the autumn and come again in the spring. It is these shoots that peep above the ground that we eat.

Asparagus will stay in the ground for 15–20 years, so the spot needs to be carefully planned and maintained. It takes a while to get the crop established.

SOIL

Although it will grow in most soils, for best results plant your asparagus in sandy, slightly acidic earth. Loamy soil is good. If you have heavy clay, try a deep raised bed with plenty of compost worked in.

Add lots of good quality compost rather than rotted manure to the soil, partly because you cannot be completely sure about the rottedness of manure, and because compost is frequently a better structure.

SOWING AND GROWING

It is possible to grow asparagus from seed, but most growers start by planting year-old crowns in early spring.

Incorporate lots of compost into your soil in autumn. This is a good place for your spent growbag material, without the roots. Then dig a trench about a spade wide and a spade deep. In the middle of the trench make a ridge out of the compost to form what looks like a long pyramid a few centimetres high.

The crowns should be placed along the trench, about 45cm (18in) apart, then cover with soil so only the bud is visible. Cover with more good-quality compost and water well.

CARE

Asparagus needs to be kept moist but not wet. Hoe out any weeds as soon as they appear and keep the plants mulched if you can. Add rich compost in early spring and again after harvesting, but do not over feed. Support early growth with canes. In autumn, cut them back to soil level and burn the foliage to ensure asparagus beetle is not in the compost heap.

HARVESTING

You need to get plenty of reserves into the plant before taking any spears. It takes about three years to start them off, and then in year four take only a few spears, then a few more the year after and then year-on-year about half the crop. Cut spears singly, using an asparagus knife if you can get one, but a long-bladed knife that slips under the soil, when they are as tall as your hand, will do.

PESTS AND PROBLEMS

Asparagus beetle and slugs nibble away at the plant. Tidying the leaves away in autumn helps. You can pick them off by hand, or spray with insecticide.

First-year fronds beginning to fall.

Aubergines

Otherwise known as egg plants, aubergines have undergone a renaissance in recent years because modern varieties are less bitter. But they still need to be grown in the greenhouse or polytunnel or against a sheltered, south-facing wall, preferably on a patio where there is plenty of brick and concrete to trap the heat. They are available in a range of colours, including white, purple and red, but black is the one that gives the best and most consistent results.

SOIL
Aubergines do not like wet feet (as the old gardeners used to say), and are best grown in a fluffy loam, rich in nutrients. For this reason they do well in growbags, but remember the drainage. Personally, I like to use ring culture pots, or deep raised beds.

SOWING AND GROWING
Sow early – February at 16°C is not too early – and keep them at this temperature until the plant is well established around May. I sow three seeds in an 8cm (3in) pot and then remove the weakest two. When flowers appear, plant into their final growing position under a cold frame or in a greenhouse.

CARE
Like tomatoes, aubergines need to be controlled in order to get the best fruit. Stop the plant from growing by pinching out the growing point when it gets to around 50cm (20in) high. Thin flowers to one per stem to ensure large fruits. Keep the soil moist at all times and the greenhouse/cold frame humid. Feed with tomato fertiliser every 10 days when the fruits appear.

HARVESTING
Keep your eye on the fruits because they can easily become over ripe. When they have coloured sufficiently, take them. They will keep for a week, no longer, in the fridge.

PESTS AND PROBLEMS
Aphids Alter the growing site each year and keep a careful watch for piercing insects such as aphids. You can water with a little copper fungicide (half strength), which will help keep the botrytis at bay.

Botrytis If ever a plant needed clean conditions it is the aubergine. High humidity can lead to fungal infections, especially botrytis. Make sure the plant is free from dead leaves, and be careful not to splash water around. Ensure fruits have good ventilation.

Beans

Broad beans

Broad beans are often the first plants we grow, and they take us by surprise when we discover we can sow them in autumn. This vegetable is both easy to grow and rewarding.

SOIL
You can grow broad beans in more or less anything. They prefer good quality loam, especially if you plant them in their growing positions. However, if you have a heavy, cold, clay soil you can grow them in pots first and then transplant.

SOWING AND GROWING
Sow outdoors in late autumn (providing the ground is not waterlogged and the temperature is above 5°C), 8cm (3in) deep. Alternatively, sow in pots in late autumn or early winter and keep indoors. Plant into their final growing positions in early spring. You can sow in spring for a later crop.

Broad beans are sown or planted in double rows – sow two rows, 30cm (12in) apart, each seed at 30cm (12in) and then another row 60cm (24in) from that if you want.

CARE
These are reasonably easy-care plants. Keep them well-weeded. Often, each double row is grown inside a hoop of taut string along the length of the row to provide support. Some gardeners find the double row supports itself.

HARVESTING
When pods ripen, collect them regularly to prevent tough beans. If the beans are black or brown at the connection to the pod then they are too old.

PESTS AND PROBLEMS
Blackfly is the major concern and broad beans can become heavily infested. Use your normal aphid regime for this.

Chocolate spot is a fungal infection caused by damp. Try spraying with a fungicide, but it may not be effective.

Mice can be a problem. Horticultural fleece is an excellent way of preventing most pests.

Runner beans

There are three parts to growing runner beans: avoid frost, provide plenty of nutrients and water regularly.

SOIL

Start in October, digging a trench two spades deep and two spades wide. Half fill with well-rotted compost. Infill with soil, and cover with black plastic for weed suppression and to keep the soil warm.

SOWING AND GROWING

In spring, build a frame of canes so you can plant at 60cm (24in) intervals, either side of the supports.

Sow two seeds per 8cm (3in) pot in April and reject the least well growing plant. The remainder can be planted out in the trench in late May, once the risk of frost has passed. From then on water and feed weekly and you will have wonderful fruit.

HARVEST

Take when the beans are about 20cm (8in) long. They are ready when they simply pull off the vine – but don't let them grow too long. The more you take the beans, the more flowers will appear. You should be able to harvest them right through to the first frosts – at least October.

French beans

This plant is frost tender and will be ruined if caught in a chill. For this reason, gardeners sometimes grow French beans in a tunnel or greenhouse in cold regions.

SOIL

French beans need a rich soil, with good water retention, and plenty of nutrients. Yes, they do fix nitrogen, but they are better in richer soils.

SOWING

In late May, sow in drills 5cm (2in) deep. Sow one seed every 15cm (6in), and thin out to every 30cm (12in). Feed and water every week. Dwarf beans do not need support, but the rest do.

Take when the pods are 15cm (6in) long at most – any longer and they tend to be tough and stringy. They will crop until about October.

Beetroot

Love them or not, this is an extremely easy-to-grow root crop. Beetroot will do well in any soil or any situation, though like most plants it prefers well draining, friable soil and good sun. It can be grown either directly in the ground or in pots. As the whole plant, from the root to the leaves, can be eaten, it is a good all-round crop.

It is nice to see them in neat rows, but beetroot will fill in all over the plot, between rows of other crops, under beans, really anywhere there is enough soil.

There are dozens of cultivars, some with long roots, some with strange shapes. The simpler the better in most cases, and 'Boltardy' is as good as any, since it does not run to seed.

SOIL
Light soils are best, slightly acid, and you can add a little compost if you like. The best flavour comes from reasonably fertile soil.

SOWING AND GROWING
For an almost year-round supply, sow indoors in February. They do not transplant well, so grow them in situ, in a cold frame or greenhouse. To stagger the crops, sow outdoors every two weeks from May until late July and you will have crops almost until Christmas.

CARE
Keep early plants free from frost, but after that they more or less grow themselves. If you sow in a drill (a single line of plants), thin them out so there is at least a hands-breadth between growing plants. This way you will get decent crops.

HARVESTING
Carefully lift out when roots are 5cm (2in) in diameter, but take only when needed as this encourages those left in the ground to continue growing. Twist off the tops 3cm (1in) from the root.

PESTS AND PROBLEMS
Black bean aphid and cutworm Cover with fleece to keep black bean aphid and cutworm at bay.
Fungal infections Weed well and try to reduce the humidity as much as possible because beetroot can fall prey to fungal infections.

Broccoli

Somehow this always reminds me of Italy, perhaps it is the name calabrese that does it. Broccoli is a brassica and is prone to the same problems and likes the same conditions as other members of the family.

SOIL

Brassicas love lime and they are best when very well-limed. They are prone to clubroot, which can be countered by using plenty of lime. Ensure the soil is firm, but well-drained, and dig in plenty of compost.

SOWING AND GROWING

Start off at room temperature in February and March in 8cm (3in) pots. Sow three seeds to a pot and keep only the best plant. Transplant into a hole lined with lime once the plants are about 20cm (8in) tall.

CARE

Keep moist, and when you start to harvest add a mulch of rich compost which will feed the plants, encouraging more florets.

HARVESTING

Harvest when the heads are full but tight. Cut beneath the head with a sharp knife – be careful. They freeze well.

PESTS AND PROBLEMS

Birds, butterflies, cabbage root fly, flea beetles Broccoli can be attacked by all these, though the damage is not usually too bad in adult plants. You can protect them by covering with fleece.

Clubroot is a problem that is best avoided by not walking on your soil and transferring the fungal spores all over the place. Grow the plants longer in pots and transplant into heavily limed holes made with a bulb planter. This way the plant is well under way before infection can occur.

Mildew and leaf spot Leaf problems, such as powdery mildew, downy mildew and leaf spot, are also issues, so avoid overwatering and remove any affected areas as soon as they appear.

Try to pick broccoli before the heads are too loose.

Brussels sprouts

You can be eating sprouts from October to April, and they are not only strong plants but prolific. The key is to firm them in if you want the best sprouts.

SOIL
As with broccoli, add lime if needed to avoid clubroot. Grow the plants in pots and transplant into well-limed holes dug with a bulb planter. A fairly fertile soil is good, but not one that had been manured for potatoes last year.

SOWING AND GROWING
For early crops, sow under cover in January and February for harvesting in late September. Most Christmas sprouts are in the ground in July, having been sown in April. You can sow every fortnight from February to June and have sprouts available for a long period of the year.

Tight button sprouts need to be well-firmed in the soil.

CARE
Over-wintering plants sometimes need support, but all sprouts are good if they can be firmed in with the heel before winter comes. If they rock the sprouts will be loose (known as blown) and although still edible, they aren't much use.

HARVESTING
Pick sprouts from the bottom of the plant when they reach 2–3cm (1in) in diameter. Slice or snap off and remove any yellowing leaves. Do not use any sprouts that are yellowing. The whole of the plant is edible, and you can collect the leaves late in the season; the tops are also worth eating.

PESTS AND PROBLEMS
See Broccoli, page 116.

Remember you can use the tops for greens.

Cabbages

You can have cabbages all the year round if you want them, especially if you use various varieties, each of which are quite hardy.

April: a dwarf-looking cabbage that can be planted 30cm (12in) apart. Sow in a nursery bed in July and transplant in October at 45cm (18in) apart. Harvest when you need them from April onwards (hence the name).

Brunswick: a huge plant – you would only need one of these a week. Sow in February and transplant in May. They need about 16_C to germinate, so bottom heat is sometimes a help if you are sowing in the coldest part of winter.

Christmas Drumhead: the name is a little misleading, as December is the end of the harvest period, which starts in October. It has large heads of blue-green outer leaves and crisp hearts. Do make sure these plants are firmly heeled in, as they have to take the brunt of the autumn gales when they are at their largest size.

Greyhound: someone said that the name 'Greyhound' referred to the speed by which it came up. There might be something in it. They have conical heads and really do firm up quickly. This is a reliable favourite for the kitchen. Sow in February for plants to be transplanted under a cloche in April. You will get cabbages by the end of June – this one really is quick out of the traps.

Cabbage growing Table

	Sow	Plant Out	Harvest
Spring Cabbage 'Durham Elf'	July	September	February onwards
Summer Cabbage 'Primo'	February indoors May outdoors	June	August to October
Winter Cabbage 'Christmas Durmhead'	April / May	July	November to the following Spring
Chinese Cabbage 'Pak choi'	May to August	Sow them in their growing positions	July onwards

Durham Early: because it is an early variety, and it comes from the frozen north, this is a good one to grow in the garden for excellent results where the weather is really harsh – though I have noticed it does not like sitting in puddles. Sow in July and August and transplant by September. Cover with a cloche in the worst of the weather to be assured of good growth. Ready from spring onwards.

January King: this is just like a savoy cabbage – purple/green and as sweet as can be. Does well in frost and is ideal for winter harvest. Sow in April and transplant in May/June. Keep well watered during early growth and it will be really good for the rest of the year. Harvest from November.

All The Year Round: as the name suggests, sow when you like (assuming you can get about 15_C), transplant whenever the plants are ready (when about as big as your hand) and harvest when you think there is enough of a cabbage for your needs. They may not be the biggest, greenest or tastiest, but they are very forgiving and will grow in almost any conditions.

SOIL

All cultivars of cabbage should be grown in fertile, firm soil that has good drainage. Use a general fertiliser on the plot before planting and add lime, if necessary, as with all brassica plots.

SOWING AND GROWING

See the table above for correct sowing time for your variety of cabbage. Ensure the earliest varieties are gradually hardened-off, or acclimatised to the outdoors to avoid bolting by covering with fleece after planting out.

CARE

Make a collar of protective material and place round young plants to prevent cabbage root fly from laying eggs. Keep them well watered and weed regularly, removing any dead leaves as you do. Use a nitrogen-rich fertiliser when the cabbages are large enough to touch.

HARVESTING

Some cabbages are harvested before they heart up, such as spring greens, so take them as you like. For others, ensure the heart is firm throughout before cutting off at the stem in a diagonal stroke to ensure rainwater runs off. By scoring a cross in the stem, a secondary crop of greens could resprout. Consult the table for when to harvest particular varieties.

PESTS AND PROBLEMS

Cabbage root fly lays eggs at the base of the cabbage and the grubs, when they appear, eat through the roots. They attach to all brassicas and are prevented by putting little collars around the plant made of almost anything, such as carpet or cardboard. The plants can also be protected by using horticultural fleece.

See Broccoli for other pests and problems, page 116.

Carrots

Carrots are the mainstay of the garden and along with other root crops they form the last of the rotation in the garden. They are grown on very well-hoed plots, with little in the way of nutrition. Too much nitrogen makes them divide into funny shapes, and while this is amusing, they are not so good in the kitchen.

SOIL
This is where the words 'fine tilth' come into their own. You need to remove stones and keep the soil as light as possible – heavier clay soils result in small, strangely-shaped produce. A layer of well-rotted compost should be applied the season before sowing. Ensure the site is well dug and remove all weeds.

SOWING AND GROWING
Sow from April onwards in drills, about 2cm (1in) deep. Cover lightly. You can sow every two weeks for a long succession. Try sowing the following:

Early Nantes: in spring
Resistafly: in early summer
Autumn King: in late summer

Sow seed thinly outdoors in October for a spring crop and cover with fleece to protect from frost. Thin seedlings by pinching them out and protect from carrot fly by erecting a barrier at least 60cm (24in) high, or keep pots on plinths or on a garden table.

A raised wall to keep the carrot flies off the carrots!

CARE
Keep carrots weed-free and never let them dry out, but do not over water. Once the leaves touch they should shade out the weeds. The more you thin them out the bigger the carrots become.

HARVESTING
Pull roots when they are 1–2cm (½–1in) diameter. You can keep the roots in the ground, with a covering of straw to keep them frost-free. They are easily kept on shelves and even in a clamp – though most allotments do not have much space for clamps.

PESTS AND PROBLEMS
Aphids Heavy aphid infestation can be a problem and simple organic measures against aphids are enough to control it.

Carrot fly is a small insect that flies towards the smell of carrots. It lays eggs on the heel of the root and the grubs simply munch away. It is said the carrot fly can reach an altitude of about 60cm (24in), but the wind can blow them higher. Consequently, it is not enough to keep a fence around the carrot bed. Proper defence comes from horticultural fleece.

Mildews may cause a problem in humid conditions.

Violet root rot Carrots can be prone to violet root rot, so ensure crops are rotated each season.

Cauliflowers

Many plot-holders say they cannot grow cauliflowers, yet just as many grow them perfectly. The key is watering and soil. Get these two right and you can easily grow caulis.

SOIL
A well-dug, well-drained soil is necessary. You need not add sand or grit, just make the soil well-draining by digging. Add a nitrogen-rich fertiliser to a rich soil before planting.

SOWING AND GROWING
Sow into pots indoors in March, adding a little lime to work against clubroot as for other brassicas. Then transplant into position with lots of lime. You can also sow in a seedbed in a drill outdoors for mid- and late-summer cauliflowers.

You can't go wrong with 'All Year Round' (a great variety to sow almost anytime) and 'Raleigh' (a vigorous variety which has a long cropping). In October, sow outdoors under a cloche directly into final growing position. Protect from frost in early spring with a fleece. You will get early summer cauliflowers from these sowings.

CARE
Ensure the soil is moist throughout the growing period to achieve the white, firm heads. From the start it is prudent to water freely. Weed diligently using clean tools to ensure good growth and avoid fungal infections. If overwintering, support with canes and tie leaves in over the curd as a barrier from frost.

Add a layer of fertiliser to promote new growth in spring.

HARVESTING
Cauliflower heads are in fact young flower heads, which open up and deteriorate quickly, so cut when still firm and dense, along with some leaf to protect it.

PESTS AND PROBLEMS
Boron deficiency Cauliflowers are susceptible to nutrient deficiencies and frost damage. Ensure soil is limed if necessary and add borax if heads are browning to combat boron deficiency.
See Broccoli, page 116.

Celeriac

It is an amazing feat that something so ugly should have such a delicate and interesting flavour. To say it is just like celery is to underplay the value of celery. Celeriac has a flavour of its own, one that gives potato mash a lift, or it can be eaten as an accompaniment to beef or lamb – but more than anything, I recently had trout stuffed with celeriac and now I want the whole world to get out there and grow this wonderful vegetable.

SOWING

Celeriac is a late-winter/early-spring plant to sow. Start it off indoors in February, so long as you can provide about 15°C of heat. They will come through at different times over the following fortnight. Pop them into 8cm (3in) pots once they can be handled. Be careful – and remember the mantra:

Use a pencil or a dibber to lever the plant from the ground, make a hole in the compost and use the same tool to lower the roots of the plant into its new home. Carefully firm in and then water lightly.

Keep the plants growing in their pots indoors until at least the end of May. In the last week, acclimatise your plants, so they get used to outdoor weather – but delay this for a week if the weather is cold. Simply stand the pots at the bottom of the greenhouse door during the day, and bring them in at night.

Monarch: has large, firm roots with white flesh.
Prinz Celeriac: produces early under cover.

PLANTING

Incorporate a lot of well-rotted manure into the soil. Their needs are simple: moisture and nutrients – but they must not be too wet. Add a little sand to heavy soils, and make it as crumbly as you can. Persistent hoeing before transplanting is important.

Plant out the seedlings – once the weather is right – at 30cm (12in) apart, and make the rows about 45cm (18in) apart. I find that two 2m (10ft) rows are enough plants for me.

CARE

- Maintain a regime of hoeing around the plants – they don't like other plants touching their roots and you get a smaller crop.
- Remove any side branches that appear, which take nutrients away from the main growing roots.
- During the summer, add more manure. Liberally sprinkle it around the area, keeping it off the plants, and lightly hoe it in.
- Don't let them become dry – especially in hot weather. But keep them from being waterlogged – this is a sure-fire way of encouraging rot. In really dry times, give them a mulch, so you can water less.
- If a cold snap is forecast, cover them up. In the winter, once the crop is ready, and you want to keep them into spring, cover them with a cloche. It is a good idea to cover them with straw and a cloche together.

HARVESTING

You can harvest from September. In August, remove the lower leaves and expose the roots somewhat. This allows the skins to harden and makes them better for storing.

PESTS AND PROBLEMS

Septoria is a leaf spot of celeriac and wild celery that destroys leaves, seeds and seedling roots. The knock-on effect is that crop yield is greatly reduced – sometimes down to nothing. This is difficult to control, but 'Prinz' has some resistance.

Celery

Celery is a hungry plant, and is usually grown on a trench like runner beans. Dig a trench about two spades deep and half fill with vegetable waste. Then top up with soil. Do this in October and leave to rot in.

When growing celery, it is necessary to keep hands and arms covered as a chemical released by the plant can be converted to an allergen when in sunlight, causing dermatitis.

SOWING AND GROWING

Sow in a propagator in March, keeping at 15°C. Do not cover with soil as the seeds need light in order to germinate. Ensure the soil does not dry out. Transplant into larger pots when one full leaf appears and allow to grow at 10°C until five or six leaves are visible. Plant into final growing positions so the crown of the plant is level with the soil. Protect early crops with fleece or cloches. Trench celery should be hardened off before transplanting outside.

CARE

Celery is easy to grow so long as you water all the time. Keep it well drained, but any hindrances to growth can lead to problems later on. When the plants are about 15cm (6in) tall, give them a feed of organic fertiliser and they will put on a spurt of growth.

HARVESTING

Snap off a stalk – if they are stringy, the plants are not ready. If the leaves are yellow, they are over-ripe. You should have celery from July to autumn. Ensure plants are well watered before harvesting, then dig up the plant and snap off the stalks.

PESTS AND PROBLEMS

Carrot fly, celery leaf miner, slugs and snails are all common pests. Check stalks and remove by hand.

Young celery needs feeding to fill out.

Store in a damp cloth – they last longer.

Courgettes

There is more to courgettes than just being little marrows. For a start they are often seedless. They grow well outside and it is surprising how quickly they come to crop. The majority of the plant is edible, from the young tendrils and shoots to the flowers.

SOIL

They like a fertile soil, with plenty of good compost worked in. Some people mulch them, but I do not because I prefer to keep the humidity around the leaves as low as possible to keep fungal infections at bay.

SOWING AND GROWING

Sow in April for early crops, in a greenhouse, and maintain a minimum temperature of 13°C for germination. I sow in 8cm (3in) pots and transplant into final growing positions under a cloche or cold frame in June. For late crops, sow outdoors directly into final growing positions, three or four seeds per spot, in June. Leave until late July for colder areas.
Best of British F1: has to be on the list of good varieties.
Soleil F1: a great all rounder.

Thin out the leaves to avoid fungal infection.

CARE

■ Water well and copiously. Feed with a general fertiliser once a month, unless the soil is particularly fertile – I use tomato fertiliser. If you grow courgettes under a cloche or cold frame, you will need to encourage the flowers to fruit by pollinating by hand.

■ The flowers set fruit quickly and then drop off. If they don't you will get blossom end rot – so remove the flowers once fruit is growing.

HARVESTING

Snap off young fruit when 10–12cm (4–5in) long. Do not allow to grow large as the flavour deteriorates with size. Remember, big courgettes are not marrows.

PESTS AND PROBLEMS

Fungal infections Cucurbits are prone to fungal infections. Ensure adequate ventilation around the fruit and remove any decaying matter as soon as possible.
Root rot Soil with poor drainage will encourage root rot. Ensure the soil is prepared adequately beforehand.
Slugs and snails are voracious with young plants. Check for damage as often as possible.

Cucumbers

Cucumbers grown in the greenhouse taste so much better than those bought from the shops, and the funny shapes and knobbles make them even more interesting. In Victorian times people invented all kinds of glassware to grow straight cucumbers.

SOIL

Cucumbers need warm temperatures, and a good greenhouse is important – however, this is not the whole story these days. You can grow them outside against a south-facing wall. Try 'Burpless tasty' as an outdoor variety and 'Picolino' indoors.

Incorporate a large amount of compost well in advance, and mulch throughout the growing period. Use raised beds in very heavy soils because the clay is often too cold for growing.

SOWING AND GROWING

Sow indoors in April. Harden off and plant the young plants under cold frames or cloches in May, or in June if you do not have sufficient warmth. You can improve your chances outside by warming the soil with black plastic and then it is possible to sow directly into final growing positions, with three to four seeds per spot.

CARE

- Cucumbers need support with canes or trellis. Remove the growing tip of the plant when they reach the top as this encourages a bushier growth. Cut out the growing point when you have six flower trusses.
- Cucumbers come in different forms, either where male and female flowers appear, or female only. Cut out male flowers, which have no fruit behind them.
- Water regularly to ensure cucumbers do not dry out and apply a general feed if growth appears to slow. Clean fruits to reduce possibility of rotting or fungal infections.

HARVESTING

If the fruit or the leaves start to yellow it is too late. Take outside cucumbers as the fruit reaches 3–5cm (1–2in) diameter, usually from September onwards. Greenhouse cucumbers are ready from July.

PESTS AND PROBLEMS

Aphids Keep aphids at bay as they can introduce viruses around the garden. Ensure all tools are clean and wash hands thoroughly.

Cucumber mosaic virus is a fairly rare virus that causes discolouration and deformation of the leaves and fruit. The whole plant will need to be removed and burned.

The knobbly cucumbers are frequently more flavoursome.

Fennel

This is an ancient plant that has followed the Romans around the world. It is a fine addition to many stews and steaks and can be excellent with fish. It looks great in the garden too.

SOIL
A fertile soil, well-drained and preferably sandy, should be prepared with manure a season in advance. Fennel grows more or less anywhere.

SOWING AND GROWING
Fennel needs 15°C to germinate, and should be sown in modules in April. It does have a tendency to go to seed, reduced by growing quickly.

CARE
A mulch will ensure the plants retain as much water as possible, but regular watering throughout the growing period is necessary. Blanch the base of the stems (also known as bulbs) by drawing soil around them.

HARVESTING
Harvest in July at soil level when bulbs are large. Leaving a stump in the ground will provide you with shoots that are good in salads. If the bulbs become longer, this is a sign they are running to seed, so harvest immediately.

PESTS AND PROBLEMS
Fennel tends to be relatively pest free.

Garlic

Garlic is becoming more popular, and is easy to grow, so long as you remember that it is planted in the late autumn and winter. Only plant cloves that are suitable for growing in the UK – don't use supermarket garlic or you will get disappointing crops.

SOIL
A well-drained, light soil should be prepared well in advance, with a large amount of organic compost. Choose a sunny spot without too much shelter.

PLANTING AND GROWING
Garlic requires a cold period of 6–8 weeks, with temperatures reaching no higher than 10°C. Split the bulb into cloves and place directly into the soil, base down. Plant them about 30–45cm (12–18in) apart.

CARE
Garlic needs to be kept moist throughout growing and a mulch ensures adequate retention of water. Keep them weed free.

HARVESTING
Garlic planted in October is ready in May, when the leaves begin to discolour. Clean and dry the bulbs and store in a cold, dry place.

PESTS AND PROBLEMS
Aphids Keep an eye out for aphids, which introduce viral infections.
Damp Garlic has problems with being too damp, so make sure the soil is free draining.
Fungal infections They get fungal infections and if you can smell garlic near the plants, there is likely to be a problem. Spraying with a fungicide is not always effective.

Kale

Leeks

This brassica will grow anywhere and is a really useful green for winter. It can reach 1m (3ft) high.

SOIL
Kale will grow in any soil with good drainage. It has a tendency to rot if too wet.

SOWING AND GROWING
Sow in modules in April to July and plant out two months later. Ensure plants are spaced at least 60cm (24in) apart, though dwarf varieties can be closer.

CARE
Water in plants but do not overwater, to ensure the plant is strong enough to withstand low temperatures in the winter. Add a nitrogen-rich fertiliser in September if the crop begins to discolour. Dead foliage should be removed to prevent fungal infection.

HARVESTING
You can take the leaves as soon as they are ready to encourage more growth, though any flower heads should be removed immediately. Harvest until the plant goes to seed.

Leeks are the best alliums for winter use, and are wonderful fun to grow. They prefer a rich neutral soil.

SOWING AND GROWING
In December, sow in modules under cover, at 10°C. Keep growing until they are about 8mm (¼in) thick. I tend to sow lots of them in a box and then plant them into their final growing positions in around May.

Topping and tailing To plant leeks, remove them from their container and line them up on a table. Trim the top 1cm (½in) from the leaves, and the bottom 1cm (½in) from the roots. Use a bulb planter and cut holes about 50cm (20in) apart. Plonk a leek seedling into each hole, roots down, and then fill with water. This is then left to grow.

CARE
A regular routine of weeding is a must to prevent infection and to ensure a good crop. As for fennel, draw up the soil around the base of the leek to improve its whiteness and sweetness.

HARVESTING
Harvest leeks when they are at least 3–4cm (1–1½in) thick, or as needed. They can remain in the ground, providing they are kept well weeded and free of diseases.

PESTS AND PROBLEMS
Leek rust is a fungal infection that is common in damp weather, so ensure the plants are well ventilated and planted on a new site each time.

Onion thrips, cutworms, onion fly and eelworm are among the other pests affecting leeks. Use horticultural fleece as a barrier against thrips and onion fly. Eelworms come where there is plenty of moisture and rotting material in the soil. This is why plot-holders of old would grow onions where there had been a bonfire the previous winter.

Lettuces

The varieties of lettuce seem endless and you can have them in the ground all year round. You can start sowing in March and stop sowing in October, but if you can sow under cover there is never a month when you cannot grow lettuce. Some varieties do not heart up, so be sure you know which you have planted to avoid mix-ups.

SOIL
A fertile soil with good drainage and moisture-retentive properties is a must for growing lettuce. Mix in a layer of organic compost if the soil is poor. Choose a sunny spot with plenty of light to promote juicy foliage.

SOWING AND GROWING
Sow under cover in January and protect from extreme cold with fleece. Thin to one plant every 15cm (6in), using the young thinning plants in salads. Growing under cover will

There isn't a month when you cannot have salad leaves.

improve the quality of the final crop. Try to plant into final growing positions to ensure roots are not damaged by transplanting.

CARE
If the soil is poor, top dress with a nitrogen-rich fertiliser. Water in dry spells to make the lettuces heart up.

HARVESTING
Take as soon as they look ready. You can cut and come again with leafy lettuces, but hearting ones are best taken whole otherwise they go to seed.

PESTS AND PROBLEMS
Aphids Check for damage.
Fungal infections Keep the plants free from fungal infections by removing decaying material.
Slugs and snails are always a problem and you will end up washing many of them away.

Marrows

Nowadays courgettes tend to be grown in preference to marrows because of their popularity in European dishes, but we have grown marrows for a long time.

SOIL
Marrows like well-draining soil, with plenty of organic matter, and a sunny aspect.

SOWING AND GROWING
Sow in a greenhouse in April for early crops, ensuring a minimum of 13°C for germination. Transplant into final growing positions under a cloche or cold frame in June. For late crops, sow outdoors in June directly into final growing positions, three or four seeds per spot. Leave until late June for colder areas.

CARE
Keep marrow plants moist and never under water stress. You may need to support the plants in wind. The art is keeping the fruits, or the plant as a whole for that matter, off the soil. I have seen them on a mound and trailing over a pallet.

HARVESTING
Removing young fruit will encourage further fruiting, though they do not store well. For winter vegetables, allow them to grow to full size.

PESTS AND PROBLEMS
Fungal infections Water carefully and don't splash it about and increase humidity. A spray in high summer with Bordeaux solution will help.

Onions

Onions are a must for all plots and quite rightly, since they are such a useful vegetable. They are the mainstay of shows and probably the second most grown plant besides potatoes.

SOIL
Possibly the best soil for growing onions is wood ash and many of the problems associated with onions can be removed by growing them where there was previously a bonfire. Soil should be alkaline and well-draining. Add a layer of organic compost before planting and dig over well. If the plot is prone to freezing, warm it with a layer of fleece before planting.

SOWING AND GROWING
- The traditional time to sow onion seed is Boxing Day (26 December) for transplanting in April. For a quicker crop, plant sets in March and stagger planting through to April for a lengthy supply of onions, 2–3cm (1in) deep and at least 5cm (2in) apart (for larger crops, leave at least 10cm (4in) between plants). Sets are treated bulbs that produce a crop in five months.
- Japanese onions are sown in August or as sets planted in October. These overwinter and produce a crop in the early summer.

CARE
To prevent fungal infections, ensure the beds are well weeded and watered. As the plants become established, stop watering to prevent the plants rotting.

HARVESTING
Onions can be harvested from August to November, or when the bulbs have swelled to sufficient size for your needs.

PESTS AND PROBLEMS
See Garlic, page 126.

Parsnips

This is an aromatic plant that stays in the ground almost the whole year.

SOIL
Think carrots (their nearest neighbour) with a slightly sandy soil and not too packed with nutrients.

SOWING AND GROWING
Sow in late April or May. Use two to three seeds per growing station, roughly 15cm (6in) apart, and thin to one plant per station. Germination is erratic, and you can wait a month before they appear. Grow them quickly and water well at first. Parsnips grown quickly produce a sweeter crop.

CARE
They do not need much in the way of care. Keep weeded and water evenly, do not leave them to dry out and then water again or they swell and split.

HARVESTING
Harvest from when they look ready – at least from autumn onwards, though it is possible to leave them in the ground until needed. You can have them in the ground for a long time – until next spring if necessary.

PESTS AND PROBLEMS
Carrot fly Protect mature crops of parsnips still in the soil from the risk of carrot fly as for carrots.
Celery leaf miner can cause damage – pick off affected leaves by hand.
Downy mildew and powdery mildew can be a problem, so ensure the beds are kept well weeded and check moisture levels.
Parsnip canker Choose disease-resistant cultivars to prevent parsnip canker.

Peas

Frozen peas have become so affordable that gardeners are not growing peas as much as they once did, but I think an allotment is not worth the name without them.

SOIL
Good, water-retentive soil is a must, so dig in plenty of good compost. Yes, peas are legumes and as such they fix nitrogen from the air, but this does not mean they do not need good fertility – they do much better with rich compost.

SOWING AND GROWING
I have always found peas do well if sown in November in a sheltered spot. Place a cloche over them to deter birds and to warm the soil when plants are young. Plant in drills with 13cm (5in) between plants and support with canes or trellis.
You can also sow from April to July.

HARVESTING
You will see the pods fill, and then you can take. Regular harvesting encourages more flowering, so keep on taking peas.

PESTS AND PROBLEMS
Aphids, weevils, moths and seed beetles that attack the foliage and pods, are all major problems with peas, but they can usually withstand a small amount of damage. Pick off any insects as you see them. Use a soap spray on aphids.
Pea leaf and pod spot is a fungal infection that has no control available, so ensure good hygiene is observed.
Root rot Ensure the soil is warm to avoid root rot and purchase disease-resistant cultivars where possible.

Peppers

From hot chillies to medium capsicums, whole books have been written about peppers. They are best grown in a greenhouse, though in the south they can sometimes be grown outside, but this can be hit and miss.

SOIL
Well-draining soil should be prepared with light, organic compost. Cover pots with cling film or a cloche to warm the soil before planting. You can use growbags, though I have found richer compost to be better.

SOWING AND GROWING
Peppers like hot germination. Some of them need 25°C and you need to use a propagator. Under-soil heating is beneficial. Generally, and for capsicums, seeds must be sown at 18–21°C for germination to take place. Keep seedlings no colder than this, then harden off and plant into pots.

I like to use ring culture pots for capsicums, 30cm (12in) pots for rainbow and smaller chillies.

Take capsicums when grown, or leave them until they are red.

CARE
Think tomatoes. Feed with a liquid fertiliser weekly as plants establish, and provide support with canes as fruit can be heavy and break the stems. Restrict the larger fruits to six per plant, but the smaller chillies can produce a couple of dozen.

HARVESTING
By picking the first peppers as they are green you will encourage further crops to be produced. Cut off roughly 1–2cm (½–1in) away from the join of the stem to the fruit. Chillies can be left on the plant until they are fully and deeply red.

PESTS AND PROBLEMS
Aphids and whitefly If you have a problem with aphids and whitefly, a control of ladybirds will help.

Fungal infections Peppers can be prone to fungal infections and need to be kept clean and have low humidity. Some books tell you to grow them with high humidity and to water the path, and this works, but I prefer to keep the humidity down as much as possible.

Potatoes

Possibly the most important crop on the plot, though these days some gardeners are questioning why we grow maincrop potatoes when space is at a premium and we could be growing first earlies. I still like to grow maincrop because I feel as though I have some food stored for winter. Whichever way you look at it, there is plenty to do when you are growing spuds.

Vegetable gardeners identify potatoes in the following way:

Earlies, also known as new potatoes, are quicker to grow. If you have only a small space, grow earlies in large sacks, dustbins or even old washing machine drums, as they will be ready sooner.

Maincrop are slower growing and larger, and can be left in the soil until needed.

SOIL
Preferably a deep soil with plenty of organic compost worked in before planting. People dig in huge quantities of manure in the winter prior to planting in the spring. If the soil is heavy or clay based, dig over thoroughly and add sand for drainage.

SOWING AND GROWING
Sow seed tubers in a drill 10–15cm (4–6in) deep, with any sprouting points facing upwards. Leave 40cm (16in) between tubers. When the shoots appear, cover with a plastic mulch (cutting holes for the plants), to exclude weeds and light and prevent the tubers greening and becoming poisonous.

Growing potatoes in straw, one of the many ways to grow them.

CARE
Ensure tubers are not exposed to light, so earth up (drawing soil around the stem to about 10cm) when plants are approximately 20–25cm (8–10in) tall, covering base leaves if necessary. If planting in containers, add a 10cm (4in) layer on top when plants are 15cm (6in) tall and repeat when a further 5cm (2in) of growth is seen.

- **Earlies**: water well every fortnight during dry weather, especially during flowering.
- **Maincrop**: do not water until the tubers reach 1–2cm (½–1in) in size. A fortnight before the maincrop are ready for harvest, cut down the foliage growth so stems are only 5–8cm (2–3in) above the level of the soil. This will improve the skins on the tubers.

HARVESTING

As the plant flowers, this is usually an indication the tubers are ready. Using a fork, dig up the plant and carefully separate the potatoes from the root. For larger maincrop potatoes leave them in the ground until October before harvesting.

PESTS AND PROBLEMS

Potato blight appears when rain falls following a hot spell and the spores of the fungus burst into life. You can grow cultivars that offer some resistance to the disease, such as 'Cara', 'Estima' and 'Kondor'.

Usually, blight destroys crops and you should dig up and burn everything. Take all the baby tubers out of the soil, so nothing remains to leave disease in the ground. Wash clothes, hands and boots between visits to the plot to avoid transferring blight from potatoes to your tomatoes.

A row of potatoes, earthed up a little and labelled.

Look out for signs of blight – blackening leaves.

Pumpkins

Pumpkins look great on the plot, and they are fun to grow, especially if you like pumpkin pie or soup. The variety 'Atlantic Giant' will provide huge fruits – they can take over.

SOIL

A fertile soil is required, with good drainage and an open, sunny aspect. Warm the soil with fleece or plastic before sowing. Plenty of water and good drainage are important.

SOWING AND GROWING

Seeds germinate at 13°C, so it is best to sow indoors in April–May. Alternatively, sow in final growing positions in June, but be aware the summer might not be long enough to reach maturity. It helps if you cloche the young plants. If the larger varieties are planted, ensure you leave at least 80cm (32in) between plants.

There are so many kinds of pumpkin – brilliant in soup!

CARE

Pumpkins set very deep roots and need less water than other members of the family, but they are helped if they are mulched. Support heavy fruits to prevent stems from snapping, and add netting around individual fruits to prevent them from sitting on the soil – a pallet works well here.

HARVEST

Pumpkins are ready when they sound hollow when tapped and have coloured up. The skins get harder in dry weather.

PESTS AND PROBLEMS

Mosaic virus Pumpkins are susceptible to cucumber problems, such as mosaic virus, so avoid growing in a spot where you know the disease to have occurred.

Slugs and snails love pumpkins, so take the usual precautions.

Powdery mildew can cause damage. Water from soil level and remove any affected leaves as soon as possible.

Radishes

There are so many radishes to choose from – mild, hot and mouli – and you can grow them almost all year round.

SOIL
A rich soil with good moisture retention is necessary. Add a layer of organic compost well in advance of sowing. Generally, any soil will do, with the addition of a little compost to lift it.

SOWING AND GROWING
Sow seed every two weeks to ensure a crop throughout the season. Sow early varieties in pots in December indoors, to be planted out in April. Other varieties can be sown directly into final growing positions from March, protected with a cloche or cold frame. Similarly, sow every two weeks until September, to provide crops until December.

HARVESTING
Summer radishes should be harvested as soon as the roots appear ready. Winter radishes can be kept in the ground until needed, but protect them from frosts and try to keep the slugs down.

PESTS AND PROBLEMS
Aphids and root fly If you want to grow radishes all year round, plant them in containers and cover with fleece to protect from aphids, root fly and various insects.

Slugs love radishes more than any other crop.

Radishes are really wonderful early-grow plants. You can use the small ones in salads and the large mooli types in curries.

Spinach

This is a great crop, though not always an easy one, and you can have them from spring to autumn.

SOIL
Spinach is one of those plants that accumulate nitrates in the leaves – sometimes to a very high level. Grow it on soil that has not been heavily manured, maybe the year before potatoes. Apart from that it will grow in most soil types, providing the soil is moisture retentive.

SOWING AND GROWING
Sow in final growing positions from January, and every two weeks until September, thinning plants to one every 8cm (3in) when they are 5cm (2in) tall, then every other plant when doubled in size. The larger the space, the better they are for cut-and-come-again crops. Crops planted in early autumn may struggle through the winter, either bolting or having stunted growth. In such cases, sow in modules indoors and transplant in March.

CARE
Water continually during dry periods. If growth slows, you may need to add a top dressing of a nitrogen-rich fertiliser.

HARVESTING
It is possible to take leaves as necessary or to harvest the whole plant around 3cm (1in) from soil level, allowing it to grow for further cuttings.

PESTS AND PROBLEMS
Birds Grow plants under netting to prevent birds from stealing your crop.
Downy mildew Ensure you grow cultivars that are resistant to fungal infections such as downy mildew, and allow plenty of space between plants to enable air to circulate.

Swedes

There is nothing on the planet worth growing more than swede – except perhaps carrot. Cooked carrot and swede with butter and pepper is possibly the greatest vegetable combination.

SOIL
Swedes require specific conditions and if you get these right you will have great success. The soil must be low in nitrogen but fairly fertile, well draining but not dry and manured at least two seasons previously. Ensure the site is open with full sun.

SOWING AND GROWING
In May, sow in drills 2.5cm (1in) deep, thinning growth to one plant per 20–24cm (8–9½in).

Ensure swedes are watered well, but do not allow water to remain stagnant around the roots as this will rot them. Weed the beds thoroughly, keeping on top of this throughout the growing period.

HARVESTING
Lift swedes when roots are 10–15cm (4–6in) in diameter. They can be stored whole in a cold dark place, or cooked and frozen.

PESTS AND PROBLEMS
Boron deficiency Swedes are prone to most brassica problems (see Cabbage), but also suffer from boron deficiency, identified by dark rings in the lower part of the root. Add general fertiliser in summer. Every three years, apply rock dust to the soil.

Sweetcorn

Sweetcorn is becoming more popular, but it is grown with varying degrees of success. To achieve proper fruits, the plants need to be kept warm and that means growing them under cover in northern climes. These days you see fields of corn in flower all over the country, but they will never set fruit, instead they will be chopped up to feed cattle.

Always grow your sweetcorn in a grid rather than a line to aid pollination – the wind blows pollen over the female flowers. If you grow in a polytunnel, keep both sets of doors open to encourage pollination.

SOIL

Ensure the soil is warmed before sowing by adding a layer of fleece or plastic during cold months. Soil should be light and in a sunny aspect. Add a layer of organic compost before covering and dig over well. Sweetcorn grows best in loam, not clay.

SOWING AND GROWING

Sweetcorn thrives in warmer areas, so it is necessary to sow in a greenhouse in April, ensuring the temperature does not

Great pollination comes from growing in a grid.

fall below 20°C. When seedlings reach 8–10cm (3–4in), harden off and plant out into final growing positions, preferably in a block to increase chances of pollination.

CARE

When plants flower, give them a good watering and keep the soil moist. Avoid overwatering to keep fungal infections at bay. Support tall plants by earthing up around the base or using canes.

HARVEST

As flowers turn brown and appear desiccated, test the fruits for ripeness. If the liquid in a grain is clear, it needs a little longer to ripen; if it is milky, the cob is ready. Harvest by snapping off the cobs.

PESTS AND PROBLEMS

Sweetcorn smut, a fungal infection borne in rainwater, can affect the growth of fruits, spoiling some aspects of the crop. Remove all affected growth and destroy, and avoid growing corn for five years to ensure future crops are not infected.

Sweetcorn is probably best grown indoors in the north.

Tomatoes

The vast number of varieties available means there is a tomato for every garden, whether you prefer the large beef-types, plum or cherry. It is possible to purchase ready-grown tomato plants to ensure the success of crops, though they are simple to grow from seed.

SOIL
A very fertile soil is necessary for growing tomatoes. It should have excellent drainage and have a large amount of organic compost worked in prior to planting. If the soil is not very fertile, add a layer of tomato fertiliser immediately before planting.

SOWING AND GROWING
Sow in March indoors, in pots filled with organic compost, one to three seeds per pot, and thin to one plant. Ensure the temperature is at least 14°C for germination to take place,

Gardener's delight in a pot.

either by heating a greenhouse or by using a specialist heated propagator. A higher temperature will speed up germination. Feed with tomato fertiliser after two weeks and transplant into larger pots or growbags to remain in the greenhouse.

CARE
Water well throughout the growing period, especially plants that are growing in pots or containers, but do not overwater, as this can alter the flavour. Add a dressing of potassium sulphate if growth seems slow or leaves droop and fall off. The amount of fruit produced can be increased by pruning (see Under cover plants: Tomatoes, page 78).

Turnips

The turnip is an easy-to-grow plant. Its root is a favourite vegetable for roasting, and the tops can be eaten in salads.

SOIL
A cool, nitrogen-rich soil with neutral acidity is required. Work in a large amount of organic compost well in advance of planting.

SOWING
Beginning in February, sow thinly every three weeks directly into final growing positions, thinning to one plant every 12–15cm (5–6in). Cloche early sowings once the plants are growing. Cool conditions are needed for germination, so do not sow when the weather warms.

CARE
Turnips prefer wet conditions, so ensure they are watered well during dry spells. Remove weeds from the bed to reduce the risk of fungal infections.

HARVESTING
As the roots grow to around 6–7cm (2½in) pull as required. You can use the leaves as they reach 6–7cm (2½in) tall, leaving 2.5cm (1in) growth for further sprouting (providing conditions are moist).

PESTS AND PROBLEMS
See Cabbages, page 118.

Fruit trusses ripen from the first tomatoes; this moves down the vine.

HARVESTING
Fruits ripened on the vine have the best flavour, so where possible harvest when fruits reach their full colour. In early October, pick off any remaining fruit and leave in a warm, clean place to ripen. The ethylene exuded from overripe bananas will aid the ripening process, though ensure the fruit does not rot so as not to spoil any of the crop.

PESTS AND PROBLEMS
Fungal infections Avoid infections by controlling humidity and removing the lower leaves from the stems to improve airflow.
Soil-borne diseases Use growbags to reduce the risk of soil-borne diseases.
Whitefly, aphids and mites can be combated using biological controls.

GROWING FRUIT

Fruit grown on the plot is far better than you can buy.

Top fruit and soft fruit

Top fruits are those that grow on trees: apples, pears, cherries, plums, cobs and filberts, walnuts, hazelnuts and quince. The rest are soft fruits: raspberries, gooseberries and currants of various kinds. Although strawberries are soft, often top- and soft-fruit nurseries do not sell or include them in their lists. Both top fruit trees and soft fruit bushes come as bare-rooted plants.

Bare-rooted fruit trees

Many of our fruit trees are planted in winter when there are no leaves on the trees. We tend to think they are dormant, but deciduous plants – those that lose their leaves in the autumn – are not dormant at all, they are simply saving nutrients and water during the winter, a period when it is too cold to make the process of photosynthesis a profitable exercise.

The real benefit of deciduous trees is that you can do all sorts of things to them and they will not drop dead so long as they have no leaves. As soon as leaves appear, the tree has to be left alone with its roots in moist soil for the rest of the spring and summer.

Rootstocks

Many trees, including top fruit, come with roots that are not their own, but have been grafted onto a root from another plant for two reasons. First, you will have identical trees to an original, which cannot be achieved by sowing seeds.

Bare rootstock ready for planting.

BARE OR BALL?

There is a difference between bare-rooted and ball-rooted trees. The former usually come in a plastic bag which has the tree branches already pruned and bare roots in the bottom, sometimes wrapped in moist newspaper. Ball-rooted plants come with their roots in a net that also holds some compost. These are usually found in garden centres and are more convenient because the balls can be watered and the tree will manage for a year or so quite happily, so long as it does not dry out.

Ball-rooted trees can be planted at any time of the year so long as you are careful not to damage the roots and you give the tree plenty of water when you put it in. Bare-rooted trees need to be planted in the winter or early spring at the latest.

On the whole, bare-rooted stock do better than ball-rooted or container-grown plants because they have unencumbered root systems that have been allowed to grow normally.

Second, the type of rootstock the plants are grafted onto affects the eventual size and growth of the overall plant. Rootstocks have names and numbers, indicating whether they will produce dwarf, medium or large trees, and when you buy, you can decide which one you want. The information is usually on the label, or you can ask. Fruit trees on allotments should be fairly dwarfing in stature, if only to stop shading adjacent plots.

MM106 (the name of a rootstock) is the main stock used in commercial orchards and, if unpruned, will give a slender tree about 3–3.6m (10–12ft) in height. The National Fruit Collection at Brogdale, Kent, is on M9, which reaches about 2.4m (8ft). Trees on M27 are not much bigger than a tomato plant and after several years of shaping, need no pruning.

Planting fruit trees

Don't wait around to get the plants in the ground. They deteriorate in warm rooms, so harden off those bought from a supermarket by keeping them in a cool greenhouse for a few days, then plant as soon as possible. If you cannot plant straight away, dig a spit out of the soil and store the root in it. To plant the tree:

- Dig a large hole, 1m (3ft) in diameter and 60cm (24in) deep. Keep the soil, removing stones and any roots as you find them.
- Improve the drainage of the soil beneath the hole – this is especially important if your soil is clay-based.
- Add to the soil 30% of the volume of really good, well-rotted manure or compost. Also add a good handful of bonemeal or other organic fertiliser (don't forget to wear gloves when handling organic, animal-based fertilisers).

- Force a good-sized stake into the hole at a diagonal. Do this first, because forcing it in once the tree is in place can damage the roots. Line the bottom of the hole with a few spades-full of the soil and compost mixture and then tie the tree to the stake with a proper tree tie – use one with a buckle so it can be loosened later (string will rub the bark). Spread the roots as widely as possible, touching the bottom of the hole.
- Firmly but carefully fill in the hole, using your feet to compress the soil. Try not to shock the tree by stamping or bashing the earth with the spade. Once the hole is full, loosen the tree tie a little.
- Give the tree a long, long drink of water.
- Try to keep the area around the tree weed-free, and do not allow grass to grow.
- In the spring give the tree a mulch of well-rotted manure and compost mixed 50:50 and treat the tree for insect invasion by spraying with organic insecticide.

Aftercare

It takes three or more years for a tree to establish itself and produce fruit, but then it will give you perfect fruit for a generation to come, so being careful at the start brings rewards later.

- In the first year, remove any fruit that appears.

A fruit cage protects your fruit from hungry birds.

- In the second year, prune the tree in the winter: remove any branches that are touching and shape the tree so it resembles a wine glass.

Do I need a fruit cage?

A fruit cage is a framework set into the ground and covered in a net to keep birds off the crop. The need for such a structure depends on how much you value your fruit, but it does commit you to using a large proportion of your plot for fruit, which might be a problem on a small allotment. You can cover your fruit with horticultural fleece, but it does not look as attractive as a cage.

TOP TIP

GROW A FRUITY HEDGE

The best adjunct to an exterior fence is a few layers of impenetrable blackberries, there for all to pick. It is an effective way to keep intruders at bay and you can stock up the freezer with fruit-filled pies and the demijohns with wine for free.

A TO Z OF FRUIT

Apples

Apples will grow on any soil, especially if you follow the procedures for settling a tree above. Aim for a good loam if possible, this way the apples will provide the best fruit: too wet and they suffer from canker, too dry and the plant cannot get enough nutrients and the fruits are small.

On the plot it is a good idea to plant apples against a fence, trained as a cordon, an espalier or a fan, allowing you to have a crop in a small space. I grew a fan-trained apple against a shed wall.

Save space by training your apples on wires against a fence or wall.

PRUNING

■ In June, trim back the lateral branches to about five leaves.
■ In winter, cut these back to about three buds, and fruiting spurs will develop. Also, cut back branches by around a third, and cut out dead wood and branches that are touching.

FEEDING

Feed in winter with a mulch of well-rotted manure, but do not let it touch the tree. In summer, give a dressing of organic fertiliser.

VARIETIES

First, consider why you want to grow apples. There is a multitude of varieties available: 'James Grieve' is a good all-rounder that will grow in a tub and will act as a pollinator for other varieties.

Familiar varieties, such as 'Cox's Orange Pippin' and 'Mont Russet', are still available today. I personally have six apples: one 'Scarlet Pimpernel', two 'James Grieve' and three 'Bramley'. This combination gives me a couple of gallons of perfect cider every autumn.

PESTS AND PROBLEMS

Codling moth and **woolly aphid** Spray in spring, before flowering, against codling moth and woolly aphid. Repeat in summer after flowering – some fruit-growers repeat every two weeks in summer.

This apple is grown as a standard on dwarfing rootstock.

Apricots

You can grow apricots outside in the south of England, especially if you have a shed to grow against. Some sites have a communal south-facing brick wall.

Apricots can be grown in a polytunnel, but you have to be sure to prune the tree back each year to keep it under control. The plant pushes out fruiting laterals on all the wood, old and new, and, if growing outdoors, you only need to trim the tree to shape.

FEEDING

Feed as for apples.

Blackberries and raspberries

Blackberries are not so easy to buy these days and do well when planted in the allotment. Raspberries are easy-grow plants, and if you have a sunny site, dig plenty of manure into the soil and take a bit of care, you cannot go wrong.

PLANTING RASPBERRIES

One of the major problems with raspberries comes from sharing plants from cuttings around the plot. They can build up all kinds of viral problems, and as they will be in the ground for a number of years, it is advisable to buy new stock from a nursery.

Usually, raspberries are bought as as one-year-old plants. They can be planted in spring about 1.5m (5ft) apart, preferably in a row along a wire support. Cut the plants down to a height of just 15cm (6in) and water well. Around each plant give a good covering of compost and add a handful of organic fertiliser.

Raspberries prefer lots of sun and well-drained soil. You could add a spade of sand to the soil to improve drainage. They like dry feet, but still need watering when fruiting. They also need plenty of organic material.

SPRING- AND SUMMER-BEARING RASPBERRIES

Spring-fruiting raspberries fruit on last year's canes, so let them grow and then cut them out once they have been harvested. Autumn-fruiting types produce fruit on the current year's canes, on new growth. Consequently, do not cut them back until you have new growth to replace them.

Always ensure you feed the plants in winter to improve the soil and maintain good flavour.

Raspberry varieties

Over the years, old varieties lose their virility and produce smaller, less tasty fruit. This is largely a result of viral infection; the raspberries of Percy Thrower's day are not around today for that reason.

- **'Glen Moy'** (early season): produces lots of fruits on canes with no spines.
- **'Glen Ample'** (mid-season): the word 'ample' is the key here – this variety produces loads of fruits.
- **'Autumn Bliss'** (late season): the best of the autumn-fruiting plants, producing a lot of fruit.

Blackberry varieties

- **'Belford Giant'**: a great blackberry.
- **'John Innes'**: a good, long-fruiting variety.

FEEDING

Feed in winter, mulch in spring and give a dressing in summer. When the fruit is forming make sure the plants do not want for water.

PESTS AND PROBLEMS

Aphids Use your favourite solution.

Birds The only really foolproof method of keeping birds off the crop is to use a fruit cage, a lightweight frame with bird-proof netting, allowing the fruit to grow (see 'Do I need a fruit cage?', page 143).

Fungal problems and **yellow rust** Spray with fungicide in June, preferably with an organic spray (I use Bordeaux solution).

Raspberry beetle grubs eat the fruit and create deformed fruit. This is easily remedied with a spray of derris.

Perfect raspberries – a summer treat.

Cherries

Cherries are not a good proposition for allotmenteers, because they are large, slow-maturing trees that take an age to produce a crop and have to be netted to stop the birds from eating all the fruit. However, in recent years dwarf cherries have become available.

There are two types of cherry, sweet and sour. The sweet varieties are those that are difficult to grow in an allotment. You need a pollinator tree nearby, if not on the plot, and you have to restrict their height.

HOW TO RESTRICT HEIGHT
Using a process known as bending, tie a string to the ends of the branches you want to keep (at least five branches) and cut out the rest. Tie the branches so they are pulling down beyond the horizontal, giving you a cherry that looks like a weeping willow.

Keep the ties in place for a year and the cherry will maintain this position, resulting in a tree about 2m (6ft) high and 2m (6ft) across, and still bearing fruit.

Feed with a good mulch of organic material in late winter and a top dressing of organic fertiliser in summer.

VARIETIES
- **'Celeste'** *and* **'Emperor Francis'**: do well on dwarfing rootstock.

Currants

Blackcurrants
A great crop, partly because it greets you in late spring when you are digging over the plot and you can smell the aroma of blackcurrant, with not a flower in sight.

The plants are bought as small bushes or single-rooted branches and should be dug into a well-manured and free draining soil. They need a good mulch of well-rotted manure in winter, and a summer top-up with organic fertiliser when the fruits are filling.

Blackcurrants almost always fruit on new growth, so once a branch has fruited, cut it out, remembering that you need to have some branches to overwinter.

PROPAGATION
You can propagate blackcurrants by taking hardwood cuttings. Simply cut out some new twigs in September, 20cm (8in) long and push them into compost to root over the winter. By the spring 50–75% of these should have rooted. By this method I was able to make a hedge of blackcurrants in a few years with little expense.

HARVESTING
The fruits are ready when the currants are full-coloured and pass the taste test, usually in late summer.

VARIETY
- **'Wellington'**: an old variety.

Red and white currants

These are treated in much the same way as blackcurrants, except that the bush has a main stem, sometimes referred to as a leg. They do not bush-up in the same way as blackcurrants and are more stand-alone plants. Allow about 2m (6ft) between plants.

Prune in the winter, cutting back the previous season's growth to about 15cm (6in) to promote more side shoots which will bear fruit next year. Keep the bush open in aspect so the wind can blow between the branches.

Feed in the spring with a large mulch of well-rotted manure and supplement in summer with a top dressing of organic fertiliser.

There are few problems other than aphids and the fact that the birds eat the buds in the winter, so keep them netted if possible.

The currants are ripe when full but firm.

VARIETIES
- **'White Versailles'**: white currant.
- **'Jennifer'**: red currant.

Figs

Yes, you can grow figs in the UK, but they do not always ripen. I have grown a large fig out in the open in the north of England; the fruits were small and nearly sweet most years, but some years they were better than others.

There are many species and varieties of figs, mostly pollinated by burrowing insects. In the UK, the variety 'Brown Turkey' is self-fertile.

They need to be grown in well-drained, poor soil, two parts loam and one part brick rubble, shale or gravel. This reduces the tree's ability to produce vegetative growth. Plant in full sun and preferably against a wall.

Indoors, plant in the same soil and train against a wall, keeping the size by pruning out dead wood and generally trimming.

FEEDING
The plant needs feeding once a month through the summer and mulching with rotted manure in winter. Water freely, both indoors and out.

At one time all you could grow were leaves, but with care you can grow fruit too these days!

CARE
The tree produces two types of fruit: largish figs and small runts. Remove the runts.

VARIETY
- **'Brown Turkey'**: best-suited to the UK because it is self-fertile and quite hardy.

Gooseberries

Gooseberries are usually sold as two-year-old plants. Plant them in the ground in winter, as for bare-rooted fruit trees. The soil should be free draining but rich, with plenty of well-rotted manure or rich compost dug in. Once in place, cut the plant back to five branches to encourage strong growth.

FEEDING AND PRUNING

In spring, give the bush a top dressing of organic fertiliser and then let it grow. Do not expect much fruit in the first year. In the following winter, trim out branches that cross each other and make the plant into a goblet shape to increase ventilation. This pruning keeps the myriad fungal infections down to a minimum.

In early summer, water freely but carefully to avoid fungal infections, do not splash it about. Cut out fruit that touch each other, another source of infection.

PROPAGATION

You can increase your crop by taking hardwood cuttings, 20cm (8in) long, from one-year-old wood, and push them into compost.

PESTS AND PROBLEMS

Fungal infections the fruits are so sweet they fall prey to fungal infections. Take care watering (see above). A spray with Bordeaux mixture in early June helps.

Saw fly Gooseberries have problems with aphids and, more dramatically, saw fly which eat the leaves so quickly you wonder how they went. You can spray in April or May, but it is not always successful. Saw fly seems to come in cycles and there are good and bad years. I have found that netting and cutting back affected plants works just as well and they recover eventually.

VARIETIES

- **'Martlet'**: mildew resistant.
- **'Hino'**: frost-resistant (sometimes new growth can be affected when the temperature is minus 8°C or so).
- **'Pax'**: not many spines and easy to pick.

Grapes

See 'Under cover plants: Grapes', page 75.

Peaches and nectarines

In the south of England peaches and nectarines can be grown, fan-trained, against a south-facing wall, but they are best grown as bushes in a polytunnel, where they should be kept well-trained and small.

Plant as for bare-rooted fruit in early winter and mulch with a lot of well-rotted manure. They come into flower in spring and are susceptible to a frost: if growing outside, make some kind of protection – plastic covering on a framework is best; if indoors, ensure there is no frost in the tunnel.

POLLINATION
Indoor-growing plants will need to be pollinated by hand – use a feather dusted between the flowers.

FEEDING
Feed with a good mulch in winter and then with a dressing of organic fertiliser in the early summer, just after flowering.

TOP TIP

POTTED PEACHES
Peaches can be grown in pots, as large as you can handle. Keep them indoors from November to May and then harden them off to go outside, in the sunniest spot you can find.

PRUNING
In spring, the tree will put out dozens of lateral branches: take out all but two per branch (they are easier to see if the tree is fan-trained). Then in November, cut out the last season's fruiting growth and, if fan-trained, train in the branches that have grown during the summer.

HARVESTING
The fruit is ready when it smells right, is firm but with a little give in it.

VARIETIES
The only peach varieties I have seen do really well both inside and outside are 'Peregrine', 'Hale's Early' and 'Garden Lady', and the nectarine 'Nectarella'.

Pears

Pears grow and are cared for in almost exactly the same way as apples, except they are more susceptible to cold winds and frost, and need a more sheltered site. As for apples, it is often best to have a pollinator tree – indeed the more varieties you have, the heavier the crop.

Trees are available, like apples, on a variety of rootstocks, and they should be planted as for dry-rooted fruit.

FEEDING
Pear trees need a good mulch of well-rotted manure that does not touch the stem, and a top dressing of organic fertiliser in early summer. Water freely and evenly during summer (never let them dry out, but never make them too damp).

PRUNING
Prune in winter, as for apples, to make an open tree with no crossing branches. Maintain a goblet shape so wind can pass through easily.

PESTS AND PROBLEMS
See apples, page 144.

VARIETIES
There are numerous varieties to choose from, both cooking and dessert types, and you can have them in fruit from July to October.
- **'Clapp's Favourite'**: an easy one to grow.

Plums

Plums are more delicate than you may think. They prefer a rich soil that is never waterlogged and has had some lime added. Keep them out of wind and if possible fan-train them against a big south-facing wall or shed.

Plant as for bare-rooted trees in the winter and give a really good mulch of well-rotted manure and a couple of spades-full of lime. Allow about 4m (13ft) between plants.

FEEDING
Mulch each winter and spring, and add a little lime. In summer, give a light top dressing of organic fertiliser.

HARVESTING
The fruits are ripe when they are full and deeply coloured.

PRUNING
Prune the tree after the harvest has been collected. Pruning is no more than a haircut, taking the tops of the growth back and pruning out side shoots where they are touching.

PESTS AND PROBLEMS
Aphids and leaf curl Spray against insect pests before and after flowering.
Canker Spray with a fungicide after flowering.
Fungal infections Thin out fruit that are touching to avoid infections.

VARIETIES
- **'Victoria'**, **'Czar'** *and* **'Laxton'***: Gardeners have great success with these.

Strawberries

With good management you can have strawberries from early summer until autumn. They can be grown in many soil conditions and they are relatively easy.

Strawberries get their name from the fact they were traditionally grown with straw under the leaves so that the fruit might not rest on the soil and become spoiled by the mud. Straw is an excellent deterrent against slugs and snails. Strawberries are also grown in pots for the same reason, with the fruit dangling over the side or resting on pebbles. A strawberry mat, a bit like a large beer mat, with the strawberries resting on it also controls molluscs.

POSITION

It is important to choose a sunny spot. They like well-drained soil, but this is not as important as sunlight. In a frosty spring cover the plants with a cloche, or even a piece of bubble wrap, as young flowers in particular seem to be vulnerable to frost even though the plants are quite frost hardy.

BUYING PLANTS

It is better to visit a nursery to buy strawberries. Posted plants can become mangled and sad, so if you are buying by post, make sure you know the company will pack them well.

PLANTING

Strawberries are usually sold as new plants and perhaps the very best time to plant them is April and May, which gives them a good growing period before having to face a winter. Plantings in September and October also do well, especially if they are covered with a cloche to protect them from the ravages of wind and rain.

Dig the soil to about a spade's depth and add a spade's worth of well-rotted manure. A good handful of grit in the bottom increases the drainage and prolongs the summertime growth if it is rainy. Plant the strawberry in this, with the inmost bud just proud of the soil. Because strawberries are shallow rooted, if you plant them high – leaving a lot of stem showing – they hardly get going at all, and certainly the root systems never become secure.

Lay straw under the leaves in May so developing fruit are not resting on the ground.

New strawberries planted in spring – notice the great roots.

TOP TIP

STRAWBERRY BASKETS

Growing strawberries in hanging baskets is a super way of getting perfect fruit. Many commercial growers allow strawberries to hang off containers suspended on a framework a metre (yard) in the air.

Left: Strawberries in a tub – cascading and free from pests.

Right: Alpine strawberries are small, but really sweet.

Strawberries grown in straw keeps them clean and slug-free.

Water every couple of days when first planted, but after a couple of weeks they should be fine. Never water so much as to cause puddles.

PROPAGATION
Strawberries develop runners, the sideways branches that will eventually produce a plantlet. In year one, remove the runners to allow the plants to develop fully. In the second year, use the plantlets to produce new stock. Simply place the plantlet over a pot of compost and anchor it down with a pebble. When the roots have formed, cut it away from the runner (if it has not already rotted off). *(See Propagation, page 58.)*

PESTS AND PROBLEMS
By the third year strawberries start to succumb to various viral diseases and do not do so well. Remove plants that are coming into their fourth year and replace them with runners taken previously. Exchange about a third of your stock each year to keep the productivity high. Also, you can introduce completely new stock, about one in ten of your existing plants, each year.

VARIETIES
- **'Honeyoye'**: this variety seems to do well in cold, damp situations and has been found to perform in Scotland.
- **'Hapil'**: prefers dry conditions and can be susceptible to wilt, but crops really well and the fruit are all similar in size and form.
- **'Pegasus'**: fine in wet conditions and stands up well to wilts of all kinds.
- **'Cambridge Favourite'**: an old variety that is still going strong. It is very sweet and will give you a perfect bed of strawberries.

HERBS AND FLOWERS

Allotments need flowers! The variety pleases the eye and confuses the pests

HERBS

Herbs are the kitchen-door plants of the culinary garden and I prefer not to grow them on the plot, other than those that look good and travel well. Often the journey from the allotment to the kitchen can be too long for some herbs. Nevertheless, the allotment is a great place to grow them, especially as a part of a rotation – filling in beds with herbs for a couple of years will free the area from soil-based pests. They also add wonderful aromas to the plot, which is good for confusing certain insects, particularly carrot root fly.

Which herbs should I grow?
Easy-grow herbs include lavender, thyme, parsley, lemon balm, sage and chives. You can also try basil, rosemary, coriander and marjoram.

Often, the easiest way to grow herbs is to buy them from the supermarket – those 'living herbs' are not much use for the kitchen, but super for the allotment to grow into something worth eating.

Sowing
In April, most herbs can be sown into modules, two seeds to a cell (or more if necessary). Cover with polythene or a plastic lid and keep warm.

To avoid damping-off, water with a spray rather than a can as it is gentler on the tiny leaves. Remove all but the best growing plant to pot on.

Pot on
Once the plants have their true leaves, pot on to an 8cm (3in) pot of soil-based compost and keep in the greenhouse. Protect from late frosts.

Planting on
Mint and lemon balm should be planted singly, in pots buried into the soil, or they will take over any other plant that might be growing alongside them. Always put some pebbles or broken crocks at the bottom of the pot before filling with compost because, as you are using soil-based compost, the drainage holes will clog up very quickly, even with the first watering.

Edible Flowers

There are many flowers that are edible. Nasturtium flowers add colour and variety to a salad, in fact the whole plant is edible.

This borage plant has edible flowers too. Try popping them into ice cube trays, filling with water and freezing them. They make interesting additions to a summertime drink. Actually, borage is one of the elements of Pimms – so why not have a Pimms ice cube to go with it?

Nasturtiums are pretty and edible.

Looking after herbs
Keep herbs well-watered and shelter them from wind and excessive downpours of rain. Feed fortnightly, preferably with an organic fertiliser. Harvest regularly, but avoid over-picking as they will need some of their leaves to keep growing.

Remove flowers that appear in early summer, as this will make for more vigorous growth, but later keep some to dry. When the weather starts to get colder, place the pots in a sheltered spot or return to the greenhouse.

If sage or thyme grows too big for its pot, transplant into a slightly larger pot and top up with fresh compost. This is best done on a bright, sunny day. Again, water well and allow to stand in a sunny spot to recover.

Mint

Mint is excellent for the digestion and general well-being and I always grow some on the plot. There are dozens of mints and they all share one irritating fact – they grow like mad! I grow them in 30cm (12in) pots of compost, which I either leave standing on the path, or more usually bury in the ground. This way I control their growth.

If you feed them once a month they will maintain their flavour.

Use mint flowers in ice cubes for lovely summer drinks.

Great tea is made by just pulling a few leaves off a peppermint plant and putting into boiling water.

Lavender

This is my favourite of all fragrant plants; I find it soothing and comforting just to know that it is growing in my garden. Lavender has many benefits for the body and mind, including relaxing properties. Applying a few drops of the oil or water to a handkerchief or to your temples, keeping away from your eyes, can help to alleviate a painful headache.

Lavender is best bought as a young shrub and planted in early autumn. It prefers a light, well-draining soil with plenty of compost incorporated. It must have good drainage, because, although it needs water, it does not like to have its feet wet.

It is reasonably slow-growing, and the temptation is to cram a few plants together to make a good display. Instead, give them as much room as possible and feed well during their first two years of life.

Feeding

Give the plants a good feed in early summer for the best blooms. I use tomato fertiliser in the water. If you grow lavender in pots, they must be watered regularly to keep them in the right growing pattern. If they wilt, and then you water them, only to leave them to wilt again, they will become woody more quickly.

Pruning

Take flowers as you need them. At the end of summer, cut about a third of the longer stems back to about 2cm (1in) – this way the plant will grow out new stems and you will avoid woody bottoms.

Lavender will ensure you have sweet flowers and many pollinators.

Sage

Sage is an easy-grow herb.

In April, sow in modules, two seeds to each compartment, and discard the slowest-growing seedling. Plant out in June. Sage gets a bit sad and woody after a couple of winters, so always sow replacements and you will never be without it.

Don't over-water: sage prefers dry soil, and full sun. Net or cloche in winter to avoid frost damage. Both these are good reasons for growing sage in pots.

Feeding

In spring, mulch with well-rotted compost, and in summer add a dressing of fertiliser.

Harvest

When harvesting sage, pull off a sprig or single leaves. Always tear the leaves rather than cutting them off.

Perfect for that sage and onion stuffing.

Basil

This is an easy plant to grow and it should be planted everywhere you have space for it. Basil likes well-drained, sunny positions with a good depth of soil. The plant will occupy a space of about 60cm in diameter and does best if the soil is neither too rich nor too poor. Grow it in pots for the best flavour – the plants will be smaller, but the flavour stronger. You can also grow basil plants from seed; plant them indoors in April and transfer them outside in June.

Feeding

Give them a watering every day – that's all the care they need. If they flower, just snip them off! They don't over-winter, so always grow new plants each year.

Harvest

Simply pick off a few leaves as and when you need them

Thyme

This is a true Mediterranean plant, preferring a warm, well-drained, light soil. Thyme needs a sunny spot, and though described as a 'hardy perennial', it is much better if you bring it indoors during the harshest of winter months – or pop a cloche over the plant if it isn't in a pot.

Feeding

In the winter, give the plants a mulch of well-rotted manure and compost mixed 50:50, and this will deal with its feed needs for the whole year. The plant needs little care for the rest of the time. Only water when it is really dry.

Harvest

Just snip at the leaves and collect as much as you need. This plant becomes woody and should be replaced every few years – you can propagate it by hardwood cuttings.

Chives

This is the easiest plant to grow in the herb bed, and perhaps the most useful. They will grow in any soil, so long as it has a little heart. They like it to be moist, reasonably rich and grown in full sun. In April, broadcast seeds into a 30cm pot indoors, then in May, dig a hole in the plot and plant the chives by removing the mass of plants, compost and all, into the hole.

Feeding
They need a little organic fertilizer in the spring, and thereafter keep them moist, but not wet.

Harvesting
Give the plants a haircut when you need to use some. Re-sow a few pots worth every year to replace aging clumps, and you can use the flowers too!

Coriander

Think about how to grow carrots, and this gives you a good idea about how to grow coriander. Prepare the soil well before planting. It needs to be soft and fluffy and raked well. Medium fertile and slightly moist are the best soil conditions. Grow in full sunlight. This plant is best grown fresh each year, but can be grown in pots and over-wintered indoors – great for winter curries!

Feeding
A light dressing of organic fertilizer in August will give the plant a flavour and growth burst.

Harvesting
Take the leaves as you need them.

Parsley

Sow in pots in March or April – soak them overnight at first. Then in May, transplant into rich soil, keeping moist but not wet. This plant likes rich soil; a plot that was previously used for potatoes will work well. Parsley is not happy in clay or sand, but a decent loam is fine. If you have sandy soil, mix in a good amount of compost. For clay, simply dig a hole and fill it with compost.

Feeding
They need a regular feed – every six weeks – to keep the leaves coming.

Harvest
Simply take leaves as they are needed.

Rosemary

This plant likes medium to light soil and full sun. It takes ages to germinate, so it is best to buy your first stock from the garden centre and then propagate new plants from this. Rosemary likes a sheltered position and you will do well to grow it by a wall. Slow growing, it can become woody after a few years, so always have replacements ready in pots.

Feeding
A light feed with organic fertilizer in the spring will be enough to feed it for the rest of the year.

Harvesting
Cut sprigs as required – cut it back quite hard in the autumn.

FLOWERS

I t is such a joy to see flowers on the plot. At one time, greenhouses would be filled with chrysanthemums, dahlias grew like huge fruits in rows on the plots and you would find roses covered with drink cups to protect them from the weather. Today, the number of shows around the country where you can compete with cut flowers is much reduced and this has had an impact on the number of people growing cut flowers.

Some allotment holders still excel at growing chrysanthemums.

Alliums rise like exploding fireworks.

Cut flowers

Alliums Flowering onions are newcomers to cut flowers. Modern varieties have no smell and make brilliant cut flowers. They are a bit like a firework – a long stem and a huge explosion in the form of a ball of colour at the end. Alliums come as bulbs which you pop in the ground in April, in a well-manured spot, and they produce flowers from July onwards. They produce great blooms year in, year out.

Chrysanthemums There are single-bloom plants that are showy and the mainstay of show types, and there are spray chrysants which produce many blooms. I suggest you buy summer-blooming spray chrysanthemums. They can be started off as plug plants and potted on from April onwards into a 15cm (6in) pot, in a cool greenhouse. By the end of May they can be easily planted out onto the plot. Remove the top couple of centimetres (inch) from the plant to encourage lots of flowering side shoots.

Dahlias Dahlias come either as tubers or as plug plants and do best in ground that has been very well manured. They have few problems during the year, although slugs and snails make a beeline for them. So long as you keep watering them and cutting the flowers for the house, they are easy plants to grow. They have to be dug up and divided in the winter, and stored in a cool, frost free place.

Roses

Roses are grown on many allotments, sometimes for show, but more usually for colour on the plot, frequently for the house. The problem is that once you have a rose in the ground, you have to set aside that piece of land for a number of years. There are dozens of different rose types they roughly fall into the following groupings: shrub, hybrid tea, floribunda, climbers and old roses.

■ **Shrub roses** produce many stems that bear flowers and generally have the appearance of a full bush. They flower on non-woody stems, so do not prune them for two or three years. In spring, remove one-third of the oldest stems, known as canes. This helps to keep the plant from becoming a poor-flowering, overgrown thicket. The removed canes are replaced by arranging about one-third of the youngest canes that grew the previous season to take their place.

■ **Hybrid tea** The variety named by Jean-Baptiste Guillot as 'La France' became the parent of all the hybrid teas. They are characterised by strong growth, large heavily scented blooms, elegant leaves and masses of flowers that last the summer. Stems are usually very thorny. Prune in late winter by cutting them down to around 60cm (24in). Cut through the wood at an angle away from an outwardly facing bud.

■ **Floribunda** are a further development of the hybrid tea, crossed with a group called Polyantha to increase their robustness and disease-fighting capabilities. They are excellent roses to grow. Prune them in late winter by reducing the height of around five canes by half, to make a vase-shaped plant. Remove all the remaining canes.

■ **Climbing roses** tend to flower on old wood, and so grow quite large before they flower profusely. They are bigger than shrub roses, but can be trained to grow as a fan on a wall, or draped over an arch or arbour. *Rosa banksiae,* planted by Lady Banks for the fist time in around 1800 is one of the best-known climbers, and is easy to control. Pruning is simply a matter of maintaining the shape of the rose, while not allowing it to become too rambling. Shoots that have flowered should be cut out to allow for new growth that will bear flowers the following year.

■ **Old English roses** are very close to the wild *Rosa gallica.* They have open faces, either cup- or rosette-shaped flowers and strong aromas. Few of the old types are available, but in 1969 the plant breeder David Austin set about breeding new roses that resembled their historic ancestors. They are easy to prune, but you will need to follow the instructions for individual plants.

Late in the season, this allotment is still full of roses.

Care

The best soil for roses is free-draining, not too rich in nutrients and deep. Dig a hole 60cm deep by 60cm wide (24in x 24in). At the bottom place an 8cm (3in) deep mixture of 25% grit and 75% soil. Mix in with the remaining soil a spade-full of well-rotted horse manure and place 15cm (6in) of this mixture on top of your soil and grit. Place your rose in the hole and fill with the rest of the soil/manure mix. Firm in well around the roots. With one exception, modern roses are grafted onto a rootstock, and you will see where the graft has taken place. The point where the shoot joins the stock should be covered by 2cm (1in) of soil.

Roses must not be allowed to dry out in the summer, but neither should they be obviously wet. They should be fed with a handful of rose fertiliser in spring and summer, and the top of the soil should be dressed with well-rotted horse manure.

With care you can have roses from early summer until November.

Problems and pests

Aphids can cause wilt, viral disease and attract fungal spores. Clear them away with an organic spray as soon as they appear in the early summer.

Black-spot is a fungal infection that spreads from leaf to leaf in warm wet weather. Remove affected leaves and spray the plant with a fungicide. The spores overwinter in soil, so cleaning it with a disinfectant such as Jeyes Fluid will reduce the problem.

Mildew is a white powdery deposit which covers leaves and buds. It also is a fungal infection which gains hold of a plant whose immune system is depleted. There are many proprietary sprays against this disease.

Rust is seen on the underside of the leaf – red, orange or yellow spots – and is linked to a lack of potash in the soil. At first sign, the leaves should be removed and burned and the plant sprayed with a rust formulation available from your garden centre. Regular feeding helps reduce this problem.

Bedding plants

Bedding plants can be grown on the allotment for colour, but also as companion plants, to fill in between rows, to disguise plants and to attract pollinators.

Marigolds are ideal companion plants. Grow them everywhere.

- **African marigolds** are favourite for planting around the vegetable bed to deter pests. They grow to over 30cm (12in) tall, and reward the effort of a weekly sprinkle of water and a monthly feed with bright orange flowers.
- **Ageratum** will grow into a small dome-shaped bush if left alone. It can be used in summer bedding and then moved to a more permanent home in the autumn.
- **Begonias** withstand neglect admirably and modern types such as 'Ambassador' are disease resistant.
- **Campanulas** have enchanting bell-shaped blue flowers and can be mixed into shadier borders. 'Purple Pixie' is a delicate variety that will seed itself all around the garden.
- **Dianthus** are also known as 'pinks' because the edges of the petals are cut as though by pinking shears. The delicious 'Strawberry Parfait' is one of the short-stemmed varieties but you can buy long-stemmed ones that are good for cutting.
- **Geraniums** are best bought as plugs or grown from cuttings, but you can sow them too, in warm conditions.

You can't beat the sweet aroma of sweet williams.

They are slow-growing plants at first, but when they get going they can take over the garden. I like to keep them enclosed in pots.

- **Impatiens (Busy Lizzy) and nasturtiums** are the foundation plants of all summer bedding, baskets and containers. They can be grown from seed in a warm greenhouse at the end of February. You cannot have enough of them, they make fantastic fillers-in.
- **Lobelia** was named after the French botanist L'Obel. These clumps of cascading blue or white plants are best sown in little groups in a tray and the whole group transplanted to the final growing position in summer.
- **Marguerites** are darling daisies that charm any border with their ray-like flowers. Plant them with **osteospermums** and challenge people to tell the difference. They are so easy to grow, everyone should have them. Choose tall varieties such as 'Summit Pink' for the back of the border, and smaller ones such as 'Mini' for the front.

- **Nemesia** is another must-have. The variety 'Sundrop' is quite unlike the other varieties in that it is bright orange. They need constant watering in the driest weather, and prefer slightly acidic soils. They do well in clay areas.
- **Night-scented stocks** are pretty to the eye, but to the nose and brain they are wonderful. Place a lot of them, 30 or more plants, in a part of the garden where you like to sit. On a hot, sultry, summer afternoon, sit, drink some wine, fall asleep and allow the aroma that forms as dusk falls to invade your nostrils and mind. There is no more beautiful way to be refreshed in the garden.
- **Sweet Williams** come in two forms, perennial and biennial. The perennial ones are usually sown in March and used as though they were annual bedding plants. The others grow vegetatively in the first year and flower in the second. There is almost nothing to beat the aroma, and the ragged, pinked flowers are extremely sweet to look at.

GLOSSARY

Associations

National Society for Allotment and Leisure Gardeners (NSALG)
www.nsalg.org.uk
NSALG is the recognised national representative body for the allotment movement in the UK. The society is owned, managed and funded by its members to protect, promote and preserve allotments for future generations to enjoy.

National Vegetable Society (NVS)
www.nvsuk.org.uk
The National Vegetable Society is a registered charity dedicated to advancing the culture, study and improvement of vegetables, offering help and advice to novice and expert show growers alike.

A

Acid soil
Soil with lots of nutrients and plenty of hydrogen ions that is acidic in nature. Combat with lime.

Aerate
To open the soil structure to allow air to get in.

Air layer
A method of propagating new plants – with a cut in a branch – either pushed in the soil or held in moss.

Alkaline soil
Often lime, this soil has few hydrogen ions in it, and is reasonable for many situations. Often needs organic matter.

Annual
The name for a plant that completes its lifecycle in a single year.

Anther
The pollen-bearing part of a flower.

Aphid
An insect that sucks sap from plants, often causing wilt and various associated infections.

B

Bedding plants
Plants used on the allotment to add colour and act as companion planting, attracting insects away from crops, *eg* marigolds

Berry
A fruit with a seed in it. Many fruits are berries that don't actually look like 'berries'.

Biennial
A plant that takes two years to complete its lifecycle. Onions are an example; they set seed in their second year.

Biological control
The process of using animals, plants, bacteria or fungi to control garden pests.

Blanch
To cover a part of a plant to make it white, or at least less green.

Blossom end rot
Where the fruit rots at the point of attachment to its flower. Often caused by irregular watering.

Botrytis
Fungal infection that affects a number of plants – usually occurs in cool damp places.

Brassica
A plant family that includes cabbages, sprouts, cauliflowers, broccoli and swedes.

Bud
A shoot, root, or flower in the making. It is usually made of cambium cells.

Budding
Taking wood with a bud on it, and grafting it to a host to make a new plant.

C

Cambium
A layer that grows in the leaves, stem, root and shoot tips, where the plant grows and repairs itself from.

Canker
An area of disease, usually on a tree.

Catch crop
A crop grown within the space of another; *eg* growing salads inside a wigwam of beans.

Chitting
Potato buds coming to life before the potato starts to grow. Usually caused by exposure to sunlight.

Chlorophyll
The green substance that initiates photosynthesis.

Clamp
A hole in the ground used for storing root vegetables.

Cloche
A transparent covering to grow plants under. Offers protection from the cold and rain.

Club root
A fungal disease of brassicas.

Companion plant
Growing a plant with another to distract insect pests.

Compost
Rotted plant material that breaks down to soil.

D

Damping off
A fungal infection of seedlings caused by high humidity.

Deadheading
The process of removing flowers when they are spent. Often encourages more flowers to grow.

Dibber
A pointed stick tool for making holes in the ground prior to planting.

Dioecious
Plants with male *or* female flowers on one plant; not both.

Division
Dividing a plant, or a clump of plants, into two or more pieces for propagation.

Dormant
An alive plant that isn't growing; usually with shed leaves in winter.

Double
A plant whose flowers have more petals than the norm – often highly prized.

Drill
A furrow in soil into which seeds are sown.

E
Earthing up
Drawing soil over plants in order to blanch them.

Eelworm
A microscopic worm, often parasitic or a pest. Used as biological control for many pests.

Erecaceous
Acidic compost – good for growing azaleas.

Espalier
A fruit tree with horizontally trained branches against a wire fence.

F
F1
A plant that has been created by crossing two plants to create a third, which has properties of both parents. The F1 hybrids are the first generation of seeds that appear. They usually do not breed true the following year.

Fan
A type of espalier that resembles a fan.

Fertilisation
The act of fusing pollen and ovum to create a seed.

Fertiliser
Substances and organic materials added to soil providing nutrients, allowing plants to grow.

Flea beetle
A small pest of brassicas that usually jump from plant to plant.

Forcing
Keeping plants in the dark so they grow either without making strong bitter flavours, or to make larger stems.

Friable
Loose crumbly soil.

Frost hole
A section of the plot in which cold air accumulates.

Fumigate
To remove microscopic infections, usually from greenhouses and polytunnels.

G
Gall
A plant's response to infection – mainly to viral infections but also other types.

Germination
When a seedling grows and bears leaves.

Graft
Often tree fruit, a shoot being grown on a particular kind of root.

Grease band
Applied to fruit trees to deter climbing insects.

Green manure
Plants grown on land to improve its fertility or structure.

Ground cover
Plants or other materials that cover the land to suppress weed growth.

Grub
A lava of insects that looks like caterpillars.

H
Half hardy
Plants that tolerate cool temperatures, but not much below freezing.

Hardening off
Acclimatising plants to life outdoors when they started life indoors.

Hardy
Plants that will survive a frost.

Hardy annual
Annuals that will survive a frost – their seeds will over-winter.

Heeling in
Using the heel of the boot to secure plants in the soil – especially as winter appears.

Herbaceous
Plants whose stems and leaves die in winter.

Honeydew
Sweet substance released by aphids, often leading to fungal infections.

Humus
The organic portion of soil – can be compost. Will enrich the soil, especially its water retention.

I
Inflorescence
A branch bearing flowers.

Inorganic
Materials made from non-organic substances.

L
Lateral
A bud that will produce a horizontal side shoot.

Leaching
Washing away nutrients from light soils.

Leaf curl
A disease of peaches and related trees caused by a fungus. Leaves curl up and then die.

Leaf spot
Usually viral, sometimes fungal, infection of roses and other plants.

M
Maggot
See lava.

Manure
Animal waste that is composted to feed the soil.

Mildew
Fungal infections of plants that leaves a powdery coating.

Millipede
Many species of non-insect arthropods that usually live on broken plant material.

Module
Trays of various shapes for sowing seeds.

N
Necrosis
Dying plants, often because of a built-in genetic trigger.

Nectar
Sugary sap produced to attract pollinators.

Nitrates
The ion used to make amino acid in the plant.

Node
The point where buds arise on a stem.

P
Pan
A dish for sowing seeds, or a hardness in the soil caused by many factors.

Parasite
An organism living off another.

Pathogen
An organism or substance that causes disease.

Peat
Semi-rotted plant material, often thousands of years old. Previously widely used as a soil conditioner but substitutes are now available.

Perennial
Plants that live for more than two years.

Perianth
The external parts of a flower.

Perlite
Mica-based addition to compost to increase aeration.

Petiole
Leaf stalk – as in rhubarb.

pH
The measure of acidity – pH 7 is neutral, acidic soils can be as low as pH5 and alkali as high as pH 8.5.

Phosphate
Plant nutrient that is particularly associated with flowering.

Pinching out
Removing the growing tip of a plant to stop it growing taller, which can create a bushy plant.

R
Radical
The first root a seed produces.

Rhizome
An underground stem usually storing food.

Root fly
A fly that attacks roots, particularly carrots and cabbage.

Root ball
The mass of roots usually visible in transplanting.

Rosette
A type of plant growth where leaves resemble a rose flower.

Rust
A fungal disease, mostly of grasses, but giving a rust-type discolouration.

S
Scab
A fungal infection affecting fruit.

Scale insect
Usually aphids; a sap-sucking insect.

Scion
A shoot that has been grafted onto a root.

Self fertile
Plants that bear fruit but need no outside influence.

Smut
A fungal disease of grasses with dark spores.

Spike
A single upright flower-bearing stem.

Spore
The reproductive agent in non-flowering plants.

Spur
The branch of a root.

T
Tap root
Single root growing downwards, like in a carrot.

Terminal (bud)
The topmost bud – the growing point.

Thinning out
Removing plants to allow their neighbours grow more fully.

Tilth
Soft, fluffy, well-worked soil for sowing.

Transpiration
The movement of water through a plant, starting at the leaf.

Tuber
A food store, mostly swollen underground stems.

U
Umbel
Flower stalk with lots of tiny stalks bearing flowers that come from a single point.

V
Varigated
Leaves of several colours or different shades of green.

Vermiculite
A mica-based additive to seed compost.

Vine
Any climbing plant with quick growing branches.

Y
Yield
The amount of crop a plant produces.